P9-BVG-805

Understanding the
Multicultural
Experience in
Early Childhood
Education

Understanding the
Multicultural
Experience in
Early Childhood
Education

Editors

Olivia N. Saracho, University of Maryland
Bernard Spodek, University of Illinois

A 1982–83 *Comprehensive* Membership Benefit
National Association for the Education of Young Children
Washington, D.C.

LIBRARY
COLBY-SAWYER COLLEGE
NEW LONDON, N.H. 03257

LB
1140.23
.U53
1983

Book design: Melanie Rose White
Original marbled paper by Il Papiro.

Copyright © 1983 for Chapter 10, "Education and Human Services Delivery," pp. 147–155, is held by Dean C. Corrigan. Copyright © 1983 for the remainder of the book is held by the National Association for the Education of Young Children. All rights reserved.

National Association for the Education of Young Children
1834 Connecticut Ave., N.W.
Washington, DC 20009

Library of Congress Catalog Card Number: 83-60866
ISBN Catalog Number: 0-912674-84-9
NAEYC #125

Printed in the United States of America.

25086

Contents

Preface

Multiculturalism and multilingualism exist throughout the world wherever countries contain regions with different language and cultural heritages as well as when countries with different languages and cultures share borders. Where multilingualism exists, multiculturalism exists as well; thus we will use the term multicultural in this book. In Europe, for example, there are multicultural areas in the Alsace-Lorraine regions of France and Germany, in the Sudetenland region of Czechoslovakia, and in the Basque region of France and Spain. North America had multicultural areas long before the first Europeans came to settle.

Multicultural education is neither a unique phenomenon nor a recent innovation. While it is becoming established within the public schools, bilingual education, its forerunner, has been a part of American public education for a number of years.

The socialization of young children into the larger society has long been considered an appropriate goal of early childhood education. While the family acts as the prime socializer, the school has accepted responsibility for helping children learn ways of behaving and interacting that might be different from those learned at home. These changes result from differences between the intimate home setting and more impersonal settings in which the child must learn to function. Children must learn to respond to different behavioral expectations: to use other linguistic codes, to function with various behavioral repertoires, and to achieve satisfactions in many ways.

For most children the move from home to school is not a difficult one. While differences in the situations are apparent to children they are not major, and much of what the child has already learned can be adapted to the new setting. While the language of the teacher might be more formal than that of the parent, it is not foreign. While the values of the school may be narrower than those of the home, they primarily represent modifications of home-held values. Thus, home and school can form an easy partnership in the educa-

tion of young children and children can move from one social environment to another with relative ease and little
sense of displacement.

However, for many children the shift from home to school
is not easy; it represents a major break. Language patterns,
social interactions, and the manifestations of values and culture may be unfamiliar to these children. In such circumstances they may find that making minor modifications in
behavior is not enough to accommodate to the school. Instead they are expected to make major changes in what they
do and how they speak, they may be forced to use a language that is foreign to them, and the social patterns and interactions expected of them may be equally foreign. These
children must not only learn their own family language and
culture but they must also learn to be competent in an alien
language and culture. Often they are made to feel that they
have to reject their own language and culture and adopt
those of the school. This can result in a sense of bewilder-
ment, in rejection, and in a loss of ethnic identity for the
child.

"Speak the way the teacher speaks, not the way we speak
at home!" "Learn to behave like a 'real American'!" These
were the admonitions that such situations often evoked in
generations past. Those of us who grew up with a home language and culture that were markedly different from the majority American language and culture were told by parents
and teachers that we must forget the life that our forbears
had valued. If we were to succeed then we were to follow
the model that was provided by our "American" teacher. All
else was to be forgotten and repressed. Many of us did succeed—but many who succeeded lost something in the process.

We have come a long way from that time, however. We
have gained insights, as citizens as well as educators and
child development specialists, about the value of languages
and cultures other than the "American" one. We have
learned that each culture has contributed to our American
heritage. Rather than forget cultures, we are learning to
praise and celebrate the unique contributions of each group.
Rather than forcing children to repress what they learned before coming to school, we are helping them to build upon
their backgrounds. We can help children become comfortable in more than one language and culture by developing

their flexibility as well as their competence. The multicultural life of the child is thus enriched rather than diminished.

With these understandings, a new role for early childhood educators working with children in multicultural communities has developed. Socialization, for example, can take on new meaning in such a context.

In this volume many early childhood educators have come together from varied backgrounds with numerous concerns to share our understanding of education and cultural diversity. This book incorporates the contributions of professionals concerned with the education of children from various cultural and ethnic groups. It represents different and sometimes uncomplimentary interpretations of the functions and consequences of early childhood education and its impact upon people of different cultural groups. We do not see the school as wresting children from the culture of their homes and immersing them as quickly as possible in the culture of the school. Instead we see the role of the school as enhancing the cultural background of children, teaching them the new as necessary without forcing the repression of the old and the familiar. The school can provide the basis in the early years for supporting cultural and linguistic flexibility in children. It is to this ideal that this volume is dedicated.

The idea for the development of this book grew originally from a preconference workshop in multilingual/multicultural early childhood education that was held at the 1979 NAEYC Conference in Atlanta, Georgia. The presentations there raised our awareness of the need for materials in this area. Many presenters from that workshop are authors of chapters in this book, although others have been included to broaden the range of materials.

The chapters in this book fall into three sections: The Nature of Multiculturalism in Children, Educational Practices and Materials, and Issues in Preparing Early Childhood Educators. All three areas must be addressed if we are to succeed in providing appropriate education for children.

In developing the conference workshop and the volume that grew from it, we must gratefully acknowledge the help and support of a good number of people. Members of the Chicano Caucus, the Black Caucus, the Native-American Caucus, and the Asian-American Caucus all helped to provide support for the conference and this publication. The

x

staff of NAEYC has also been most helpful and we should acknowledge their help, especially that of Marilyn Smith, J. D. Andrews, and Janet Brown. Finally we wish to acknowledge the support of the many members of NAEYC who have shared their concern about providing opportunities for multicultural education for young children.

Olivia N. Saracho
College Park, Maryland

Bernard Spodek
Champaign, Illinois

I

The Nature of Multiculturalism in Children

Olivia N. Saracho
Frances Martinez Hancock

1

Mexican-American Culture

Sociocultural factors affect every aspect of human development. These factors include childrearing practices, family styles, sociolinguistic patterns, and political and economic systems as well as socialization and behavior patterns. Because of their influence on the development of children cultural differences must be recognized, understood, respected, and accepted by educators.

One of the largest cultural groups in the United States is the Mexican-American group that includes approximately five-and-one-half million people (Stone 1971). Mexican Americans have perceived themselves as America's forgotten minority. Although society has labeled us as passive, we are playing an increasingly vital role in the industrial, agricultural, artistic, intellectual, and political life of the country. We are sharing our Mexican-American historical and recent accomplishments with our children—facts that were distorted or ignored for a long time. Our ancestors contributed to the development of the Southwest, especially those areas which now constitute the states of New Mexico and California. An understanding of our shared culture can enhance early childhood teachers' sensitivity to what our children bring to school.

Mexican-American culture

Culture is an elusive concept. One definition is that a society's culture consists of whatever it is one has to know or believe in order to operate in a manner acceptable to its members, and to do so in any role they accept for any of themselves. . . . Culture is not a material phenomenon; it does not consist of things, people, behavior, or emotions. It is rather an organization of these things. It is the forms of things that people have in mind, their models for perceiving, relating, and otherwise interpreting them. (Goodenough 1957, p. 167)

Spradley (1972) suggests that the concept of culture has been misunderstood because it has so many overlapping and contradictory meanings:

> Perhaps the meaning which has had the widest usage involves an *omnibus definition:* culture is almost everything. It is emotions and works of art; it is behavior, beliefs, and institutions; it includes what people know, feel, think, make, and do. (p. 6)

Culture as used here refers to life style and includes language, diet, dress, social patterns, and ethnicity. Some cultural components are geography, history, architecture, religion, folk medicine, diet, art, music, dance, and socialization practices.

One of the major obstacles which has impeded the development of a coherent educational policy for Mexican Americans is the idea that this population is a homogenous group, characterized by low economic status and low educational achievement. The focus on average economic status and average educational achievement has distorted the heterogeneity of our group in many important spheres of life. In addition, social scientists have failed to describe the diversity of our child socialization practices and their effects on the personality and behavior development of individuals. This information is vital for anyone attempting to develop educational programs and/ or policy for Mexican Americans. Even the terms that denote this group's members vary from one region of the country to another. For example, those of Mexican descent in northern New Mexico and southern Colorado call themselves Spanish Americans, while others call themselves Latin Americans, Chicanos, Hispanos, Spanish-speaking, La Raza, and Americans of Mexican descent (Ramírez and Castañeda 1974).

The historical, genetic, and cultural background of Mexican Americans is also heterogenous. According to Ramírez and Castañeda (1974), the Spanish and Indian heritage of Mexican Americans may range from none to 100 percent. The Spaniards who came to Mexico varied in cultural origin. They included individuals of Iberian, Greek, Latin, Visigoth, Moroccan, Phoenician, Carthaginian, and other backgrounds. The native

Mexicans represented distinct groups differing physically, socially, economically, and culturally from one another. Hence, the diversity. Although Mexican Americans have a diverse background, there still persists an image in the general population that depicts us as old and as agricultural workers. Contrary to this idea, Ramírez and Castañeda (1974) assert that 80 percent of the Mexican-American population lives and works in urban areas and that we are one of America's youngest population groups.

Family ties

Mexican Americans' family roles are based on the family's basic human needs, and on perceptions and functions of the family. Family relationships, leisure time activities, and the Catholic church are valued. Rituals associated with religious or national holidays as they were celebrated in Mexico are often retained. Among the folkways and characteristic patterns of action that many, but not all, Mexican Americans hold is the acceptance of authority in the home, church, and state; maintenance of personal loyalty to friends; sensitivity to praise and criticism; and the practice of folk medicine. Mexican Americans vary significantly in economic condition and social status.

Many of the values of traditional Mexican-American culture are like those of other ethnic groups, differing greatly from values usually presented in the school. (*Traditional* refers to values characteristic of communities that are rural, that are located close to the Mexican border, and in which the majority of the population is Mexican American.) These traditional values most nearly approximate the core of values which affect the behavior of Mexican Americans despite changes that have occurred due to assimilation and the impact of external variables (Ramírez and Castañeda 1974).

Teachers have been heard to say, "If Mexican-American children are to be successful in this society, they must be competitive, assertive, and learn to look out for themselves." However, our family ties focus on cooperation rather than competition. Traditionally, the culture of the Mexican American instills in the child a strong sense of extended family ties, including all relatives. Each person's identity is closely related to the family. Traditional Mexican-American families are becoming less common and most of our children are growing up in transitional families:

> Minority group families run the gamut from the traditional to the
> highly acculturated. Between these poles, all number of possible
> variations and transitional culture exist . . . (Carter 1971a, p. 226)

Since the value attached to the family is strong, there is a
greater emphasis on cooperation among the family group than
on competition, and socialization practices support cooperation. In planning a program for children of this background, a
teacher can focus on the meaning of the children's family and
their motivation to achieve for their family's sake. Teachers
can plan activities that involve the child's family in the child's
learning and that use cooperative behavior in the classroom.

Interpersonal relationships

Mexican Americans are generally sensitive to others' feelings and observe rules of conduct such as respect for the status
of others. Age and sex are important determinants of roles and
status in our culture. Older people hold more status and are
afforded more respect than others in the community. They are
respected for their knowledge of the history of the community
and ethnic group and for having more experience in life (Ramírez and Castañeda 1974). Parents especially are accorded
much respect and children are taught to respect all elders.

Within the family, roles are assigned by age. The eldest child
is given more responsibility and status is determined by how
well the child fulfills responsibilities. Older children may be
responsible for the socialization of younger ones in large families. Children and young adults who have learned their social
roles and behaviors are often characterized as being *bien ed-
ucado*. Being socially well educated is more important than
being academically well educated. Those who fulfill their roles
and know how to behave properly bestow honor on their family
in the eyes of the community.

Religion

The Mexican Catholic ideology represents a blend of European and Indian religious ideas and practices. Mexican
Catholicism supports and reinforces the values of the Mexican-American culture. Identification with the ethnic group is
reinforced through the worship of the Virgin of Guadalupe,
the religious symbol of La Raza. Furthermore, identification
with the community is reinforced by the emphasis on religious
ceremonies that are built on close family ties. Parents and

other adults are seen as representatives of God; to disobey them is a transgression against God (Ramírez and Castañeda 1974).

Educational implications

Carter (1971b) claims that lower school achievement and fewer years of schooling that are characteristic of many Mexican Americans can be attributed to three complex and interrelated sets of factors:

1. The nature of the diverse Mexican-American sub-cultures and the socialization afforded Mexican-American children;
2. The kind and quality of formal education available to Mexican Americans; and
3. The nature of the local and regional social systems and the equal or unequal opportunity they afford the minority group. (p. 275)

The majority of educators stress only the first factor in explaining the low status, suggesting that lack of assimilation and acculturation and resulting school failure are due to the group's culture. This theory is widely accepted because it exonerates society and school. On the other hand, low status and the continued foreignness of minority groups are situations caused by many social and economic factors within society as well as by cultural characteristics of the minority group. Nevertheless, American society generally blames minority groups as the cause of their own problems (Carter 1971b).

Saville-Troike (1973) emphasizes how important it is for teachers to accept and use student's cultural and linguistic experiences in establishing educational goals. This requires an understanding and appreciation of the nature of specific languages and cultural attitudes that influence the students' cognitive growth and socialization process. Zamora (1975) suggests that Spanish-speaking teachers often ask, "What Spanish shall I teach?" referring to dialects of the language. She responds that we should begin instruction in the vernacular that the children know and use. Teachers must accept children including their language system in order to promote learning.

The child's self-image is also based in culture. The child raised in the traditional Mexican-American community has been socialized within a language, heritage, set of cultural values, and predominant teaching style unique to that system.

The child will develop communication, learning, and motivational styles consistent with that socialization. When Mexican-American children first enter an early childhood program, they may be expected to function in a sociocultural system whose practices relating to language and heritage, cultural values, and teaching styles are different from those they experience at home. They must be given time and enough opportunities to explore and to understand a new cultural world.

Mexican-American children must learn to function effectively in the mainstream of the American cultural world and simultaneously continue to function effectively in and contribute to the Mexican-American cultural world. Born into a Mexican-American culture, children acquire socially meaningful behaviors, one of which is language. Language (Spanish and its variants) assists children to integrate the patterns of everyday life in their homes. Children learn appropriate ways to interact with others. Without being directly taught, they learn by looking, by touching, and by having people react to them. The active process of building the new on the old is a form of self-regulation. Children play active roles throughout this process through imitation and practice.

Children's language provides the key to development of a socially adequate identity. Children will understand what they can do and how others interpret what they can do. Respect for what children bring to the school setting should be the basis for building a learning environment that will motivate children to learn. The motivation to learn something as complex as another culture and language is critical to success (Guskin 1976). Gardner and Lambert (1972) have shown how students' motivation may vary according to family background, social class, societal values, and political and economic events.

Cárdenas and Cárdenas (1973) suggest that there are incompatibilities between typical schools and atypical children in five major categories: poverty, culture, language, mobility, and perceptions. Schools must make philosophical, pedagogical, and organizational changes to respond to the needs of the atypical child. Zamora (1975) offers a schema for designing appropriate educational responses. She suggests that schools review each of the areas of incompatibility by analyzing the problem, determining the attitude that must be developed, and determining the skills that will be necessary for responding positively to the incompatibilities. In reference to culture, Zamora

(1976) analyzes the problem in the traditional school which values conformity and acculturation and which fails to recognize the beauty of cultural diversity. In addition, teachers often do not know how to provide cultural reinforcement. In the development of attitudes, schools must be sensitive to the culture of their students. The skills teachers need to develop include: knowing how to reinforce home culture, knowing how to adapt curriculum materials to make them more relevant, knowing how to build a curriculum based on children's lives and language experiences, and knowing how to involve parents in the educational experience. The traditional curriculum is oriented to an ethnic group and culture incompatible with the culture of the minority. Children who have been called *culturally disadvantaged* in reality have been *culturally different*.

Educational approaches

Approaches that need to be developed for the education of Mexican-American children should be consistent with the children's cultural background. Arciniega (1971) has classified such approaches in relation to the causes of the Mexican-American students' life styles and their educational consequences (see Table 1.1).

Arciniega (1971) views culture as persistent and self-perpetuating with patterns being transmitted from one generation to the other. He suggests that fundamental modifications should be made in educational programs to meet the needs of the Mexican-American culture as outlined in the summary below.

1. Schools need to develop a commitment to a pluralistic model of society. Schools have advocated the myth of a *melting pot* and the rhetoric of *equal opportunities*, creating failure in the education of the Mexican Americans.
2. Schools need to be organized as a microcosm of the *ideal* society in which diversity is perceived as a source of strength.
3. In designing programs, schools need to focus on the teacher's and family's influence on the student. Teachers' acceptance of the child's cultural and family background, for example, may enhance [her or] his positive self-concept, while the teacher's rejection may diminish it. The interactions and learning experiences provided within the curriculum need to be responsive to the student's family and cultural background.
4. Schools need to recognize that children from both low and high

Table 1.1. Classification of approaches to the education of Chicanos according to the perceived determinants and consequences of Chicano student life styles.

Consequences of Chicano student life styles seen as chiefly:	
Positive	*Negative*
1. Educational system which views Chicano students as "noble poor"	2. Educational system which views Chicano students as "pathological"
Goals: Promotion, enhancement, and glorification of Mexican and Chicano culture and life styles	**Goals:** Elimination of the cultural deficiencies brought from home and peer group by the Chicano student and inculcation of middle-class values of the majority culture.
Means: Separatist strategies designed to secure community control of education. Only Chicanos can shape valid educational programs for Chicanos. Separate schools with Spanish as the primary language.	**Means:** Compensatory education designed to overcome cultural deprivation.

Causes of Chicano life styles are seen as chiefly: *Internal*

Table 1.1. continued

Consequences of Chicano student life styles seen as chiefly:	
Positive	*Negative*
3. Education system which views Chicano students as "copers" **Goals:** The development of a society based on cultural pluralism. The educational system should be restructured to provide programs which: (1) provide the basic knowledge, skills, and political awareness to adequately (2) promote constant institutional changes designed to improve the opportunity structure. **Means:** Bilingual/bicultural education for all students which recognizes the functional aspects of both cultures and equips students to deal with the societal institutions while working to change them.	4. Educational system which views Chicano students as "the oppressed" **Goals:** Complete restructuring of the educational system along with the political and economic system to equalize wealth and power in society. **Means:** Development of programs which reinstate the worth of the Chicano culture and overcome their condition of internal colonialism. Education must be organized to liberate Chicanos from their oppressed conditions. Basic changes in the economic and political systems must also be made because these affect the educational system.

Causes of Chicano life styles are seen as chiefly: External

From the book, *Chicanos and Native Americans*, by Rudolph O. de la Garza, Z. Anthony Kruszewski, and Tomás A. Arciniega. © 1973 by Prentice-Hall, Inc. Published by Prentice-Hall, Inc., Englewood Cliffs, NJ 07632. Originally presented by Tomás A. Arciniega at the Conference on Mexican-Americans, Austin, Texas, November 3–5, 1971.

socioeconomic backgrounds benefit from being educated in an integrated, interethnic setting. Such a setting would allow genuine communication across social, racial and ethnic boundaries.
5. Schools need to use the wide range of cultural resources, including human resources, in planning and implementing the young child's learning experiences. When aspects of the Mexican-American culture are incorporated into the school experience the educational goals of the school become more relevant to children from that culture.
6. Most Mexican Americans have not been integrated into the dominant society. Schools can take the initiative in working with other social agencies to develop systems that will open opportunities for Mexican Americans to become equal members of our society.

Many of these suggested changes will be resisted by some groups. Overcoming this resistance is a challenge for educators who strongly believe in equality of educational opportunity.

Laosa (1977) states that there is wide variability within any one ethnic or cultural group and one may find individual instances of deficiencies in any group. He cautions against equating cultural characteristics with deficiencies or mistakenly defining as a deficiency a characteristic that may really represent a cultural difference. He cites the Lesser, Fifer, and Clark (1965) study which shows that children from different ethnic groups may possess different patterns of abilities, learning styles, and problem solving. Each ethnic group bears its own strengths and, regardless of ethnic group, low socioeconomic status (SES) children perform less well than middle SES children. Few educationally relevant characteristics associated with ethnic group membership have been identified.

Nevertheless, the findings lend support to the hypothesis that there are discontinuities between the early environments of minority children and the environments they meet in school which appear to explain early academic failure. Laosa's (1977) research reveals that children's environments show quite unique characteristics depending on children's membership in particular sociocultural groups and that even within these groups there is much variability. Laosa finds that Mexican-American and Anglo-American mothers of the same SES use very different teaching strategies; for example, Mexican-American mothers did more teaching by modeling while Anglo-American mothers did more teaching verbally.

Ethnic differences that reflect cultural values are closely related to teaching strategies. Ramírez and Castañeda (1974) indicate that helping teachers understand the cultural values of Mexican Americans is not enough. They stress the importance of familiarizing teachers with the teaching styles of Mexican-American parents so that they can match their own teaching strategies to the learning styles of Mexican-American children.

Teaching strategies

Individuals actively strive, under any circumstances, to structure and restructure their lives in pursuit of meaning, and we must take this into account in planning children's educational programs. Teachers need to use strategies that do not demean children's culture.

For example, while teachers would not be expected to teach folk medicine to Mexican-American children, teachers can be expected to accept what children relate concerning their families' beliefs about folk medicine. A teacher would be acting in a way that would be detrimental to identity development by belittling a child or the parents by saying that a belief such as *mal de ojo* (evil eye) is superstitious.

The fact that people hold what may be regarded as bizarre beliefs for reasons that are empirically and logically unacceptable does not mean that they are therefore illogical or childlike in mentality (Goodenough 1957). These beliefs may be valued on logical and empirical grounds for a variety of social and emotional reasons. A belief, which is a proposition accepted as true, may be held in spite of empirical evidence to the contrary for reasons that have nothing to do with its predictive utility. Other things predispose people to particular beliefs such as the greater experience and wisdom of elders. Some beliefs are self-validating in that, believing something to be true, people act in such a way as to make their future experiences consistent with their beliefs. For example, beliefs about human character and motives often work in self-validating ways. Propositions that provide emotional gratification also invite belief. Many religious beliefs function in this manner as do beliefs about people and nature. In the case of the Mexican-American culture, there is a belief in *mandas*, a promise of something to a saint, either a good deed or giving up something that one values, in return for a special favor, especially in time of crisis or desperate situations (Goodenough 1971).

Another component of culture is diet, which can find its place in the classroom through cooking and nutrition education activities. In the preparation of Mexican-American food, a child's self-concept as well as home culture is reinforced. Children can bring recipes or ingredients from home to foster responsibility. Some of the skills to be learned in cooking include following directions, measuring, mixing, dividing, and sharing. When children bring in recipes, they can see the relationship between speech and written language.

All cultures teach children rules and values that justify their own actions. Proverbs, myths, stories, and fables provide evidence of public values and of their fit or lack of fit with private sentiments (Goodenough 1971). Teachers can provide children the proper setting and encourage role-playing of stories and fables that are part of the Mexican-American oral literature. Children can be encouraged to relate stories about their own experiences. Their parents can be invited to narrate stories or legends from the Mexican-American oral tradition. Children can be encouraged to observe art in everyday life, in the dress, jewelry, pottery, and other forms of expression found throughout the community. Children can be introduced not only to the traditional music and dances of their culture but also to the contemporary expressions heard and seen in their social functions.

Conclusion

To foster a democratic society, educators must educate individuals in the context of cultural pluralism. A democratic society requires that individual differences be respected and each person's education be developed through one's own life history and unique characteristics. Programs based upon cultural pluralism must be implemented to affirm the rights of individuals and their personal dignity. Only then can schools provide the cornerstone of a real democracy built upon cultural pluralism.

References

Arciniega, T. "Toward a Philosophy of Education for the Chicano: Implications for School Organizations." Paper presented at the Conference on Mexican-Americans, Austin, Texas, November 3–5, 1971.

Cárdenas, B., and Cárdenas, J. "Bright-Eyed, Bilingual, Brown, and Beautiful." *Today's Education* 62, no. 2 (1973): 49–51.

Carter, T. "Mexican Americans in School: A History of Educational Neglect." In *Five Heritages: Teaching Multi-Cultural Populations,* ed. J. C. Stone. New York: Van Nostrand-Reinhold, 1971a.

Carter, T. "Where To from Here?" In *Five Heritages: Teaching Multi-Cultural Populations,* ed. J. C. Stone. New York: Van Nostrand-Reinhold, 1971b.

de la Garza, R. O.; Kruszewski, Z. A.; and Arciniega, T. A. *Chicanos and Native Americans.* Englewood Cliffs, N.J.: Prentice-Hall, 1973.

Gardner, R. C., and Lambert, W. E. *Attitudes and Motivation in Second-Language Learning.* Rowley, Mass.: Newbury House, 1972.

Goodenough, W. "Cultural Anthropology and Linguistics." In *Report of the Seventh Annual Round Table Meeting on Linguistics and Language Study.* Monograph Series on Languages and Linguistics, no. 9. Washington, D.C.: Georgetown University, 1957.

Goodenough, W. *Culture, Language and Society. Module in Anthropology,* no. 7. Reading, Mass.: Addison-Wesley, 1971.

Guskin, J. T. "What the Child Brings and What the School Expects: First and Second Language Learning and Teaching in Bilingual-Bicultural Education." In *The Bilingual Child, Research and Analysis of Existing Educational Themes,* ed. A. Simões, Jr. New York: Academic Press, 1976.

Laosa, L. M. "Socialization, Education, and Continuity: The Implications of the Sociocultural Context." *Young Children* 32, no. 5 (1977): 21–27.

Lesser, G. S.; Fifer, G.; and Clark, D. H. "Mental Abilities of Children from Different Social Class and Cultural Groups." *Monographs of the Society for Research in Child Development* 30, no. 4 (1965).

Ramírez, M., III, and Castañeda, A. *Cultural Democracy, Bicognitive Development, and Education.* New York: Academic Press, 1974.

Saville-Troike, M. *Bilingual Children: A Resource Document.* Arlington, Va.: Center for Applied Linguistics, 1973.

Spradley, J. P. "Foundations of Cultural Knowledge." In *Culture and Cognition: Rules, Maps and Plans,* ed. J. P. Spradley. San Francisco: Chandler, 1972.

Stone, J. C. "The Mexican-American Heritage." In *Five Heritages: Teaching Multi-Cultural Perspectives,* ed. J. C. Stone. New York: Van Nostrand-Reinhold, 1971.

Zamora, G. "When Spanish Is the Native Language." In *Proceedings of the First Inter-American Conference on Bilingual Education,* ed. R. Troike and N. Modiano. Arlington, Va.: Center for Applied Linguistics, 1975.

Zamora, G. "Staff Development for Bilingual Bicultural Programs: A Philosophical Base." In *Bilingual Schooling in the United States, a Sourcebook for Educational Personnel,* ed. F. Cordasco. New York: McGraw-Hill, 1976.

Janice Hale

Black Children:
Their Roots, Culture, and Learning Styles

DuBois (1903) describes the Black person in America as possessing two "warring souls." Black people are products of their Afro-American heritage and culture. However, they are also shaped by the demands of Anglo-American culture. Those who share the spirituality of the Black experience share it mentally and emotionally. Black people transform every cultural mode they interact with: language, music, religion, art, dance, problem solving, sports, writing, or any other areas of human expression.

The purpose of this article is to describe this spirituality or "soulfulness" and to demonstrate its relationship to the cognitive development of Black children, including the conflict that ensues when Black children are evaluated from an Anglocentric framework.

Cultural style

Hilliard (1976) sets forth some basic assumptions about human behavioral styles, or the framework from which people view the world. He reviews several styles, and concludes that "every style is necessary, valuable and useful in human experience if society is to function fully" (p. 43). While style is evident in all areas of an individual's behavior, one can learn aspects of other styles. Hilliard also states that strong relationships exist between style and socioeconomic level and between style and cultural or ethnic group membership. He finds no evidence, however, of a relationship between basic intelligence and style.

Elements of Afro-American cultural style are also identified by Hilliard (1976). He states that Afro-American people—

- tend to view things in their entirety and not in isolated parts;
- seem to prefer inferential reasoning rather than deductive or inductive reasoning;
- Tend to approximate space, number, and time instead of aiming for complete accuracy;
- appear to focus on people and their activities rather than objects. Many Black students have chosen careers in the helping professions even though these types of jobs are scarce and the curriculum is rigorous.
- have a keen sense of justice and quickly perceive injustice;
- tend to prefer novelty, personal freedom and distinctiveness, such as in music and styles of clothing;
- in general tend not to be "word" dependent, but are proficient in nonverbal as well as verbal communication.

Akbar (1975) describes the Afro-American child (see Table 2.1).

Cohen (1971) delineates two styles of learning and of schools in terms of differences in methods for selecting and classifying information. Hilliard (1976) summarizes the characteristics of the analytical and relational styles (see Table 2.2).

Most schools require an analytical approach to learning (Cohen 1971). Children who function with a different cognitive style or who have not developed analytical skills will be poor achievers early in school and will do worse as they move to higher grade levels.

Not only does the school reward development of the analytic style of processing information, but the overall ideology and environment of the school reinforces behaviors associated with that style.

> Aspects of analytic style can be found in the requirements that the pupil learn to sit increasingly long periods of time, to concentrate alone on impersonal learning stimuli, and to observe and value organized time-allotment schedules. (Cohen 1971, p. 829)

The differences between children who function with relational and analytic styles is so great that children whose cognitive organization is relational are unlikely to be rewarded with grades regardless of their native ability, the extent of their

Table 2.1. The Afro-American child.

Is highly affective
Uses language requiring a wide use of many coined interjections
(sometimes profanity)
Expresses herself or himself through considerable body language
Relies on words that depend upon context for meaning and that
have little meaning in themselves
Prefers using expressions that have several connotations
Adopts a systematic use of nuances of intonation and body
language such as eye movement and positioning
Prefers oral-aural modalities for learning communication
Is highly sensitive to others' nonverbal cues
Seeks to be people oriented
Is sociocentric
Uses internal cues for problem solving
Feels highly empathetic
Likes spontaneity
Adapts rapidly to novel stimuli (Akbar in Hilliard 1976, p. 39)

Table 2.2. Analytical and relational cognitive styles (compiled from Rosalee Cohen).

Analytical style

Stimulus centered
Parts-specific
Finds non-obvious attributes
Abstracts common or generalizable principle of a stimulus
Notices formal properties of a stimulus that have relatively stable and long lasting meanings
Ignores the idiosyncratic
Extracts from embedded context
Names extracted properties and gives them meaning in themselves

Relationships tend to be linear
Relationships which are noticed tend to be static and descriptive other than functional or inferential
Relationships seldom involve process or motivation as a basis for relations
Perception of conceptual distance between observers and observed
An objective attitude—a belief that everything takes place "out there" in the stimulus

Analytical style	Relational style
	Self-centered
	Global
Stimulus viewed as formal, long lasting and relatively constant, therefore there is opportunity to study it in detail	Fine descriptive characteristics
	Identifies the unique
	Ignores commonalities
	Embedded for meaning
Long attention span	Relevant concepts must have special or personal relevance to observer
Long concentration span	
Greater perceptual vigilance	
A reflective attitude and relatively sedentary nature	Meanings are unique depending upon immediate context
Language style is standard English of controlled elaboration	
	Generalizations and linear notions are generally unused and devalued
Language depends upon relatively long lasting and stable meanings of words	
Language depends upon formal and stable rules of organization	Parts of the stimulus and its non-obvious attributes are not given names and appear to have no meaning in themselves
Communications are intended to be understood in themselves, i.e., without dependence upon non-verbal cues or idiosyncratic context	Relationships tend to be functional and inferential
	Since emphasis is placed on the unique and the specific, global and the discrete, on notions of difference rather than on variation or common things, the search for mechanism to form abstract generalizations is not stimulated
"Parts of speech" can readily be seen in nonsense sentences	
Analytic speech characterized by "hesitation phenomena," pauses for verbal planning by controlled vocal modulation and revision of sentence organization to convey specific meaning, since words have formal meanings	Responses tend to be affective
	Perceived conceptual distance between the observer and the observed is narrow
Sometimes view of self expressed as an aspect of roles such as function to be performed	The field is perceived as responding to the person
	The field may have a life of its own
View of self tends to be in terms of status-roles	Personification of the inanimate

Relational style

Distractable
Emotional
Over involved in all activities
Easily angered by minor frustrations
Immediacy of response
Short attention span
Short concentration span
Gestalt learners
Descriptive abstraction for word selection
Words must be embedded in specific time bound context for meaning
Few synonyms in language
Language dependent upon unique context and upon many interactional characteristics of the communicants on time and place, on inflection, muscular movements and other non-verbal cues
Fluent spoken language
Strong colorful expressions
Wide range of meaningful vocal intonation and inflection
Condensed conditions sensitivity to hardly perceptible variations of mood and tone in other individuals and in their surroundings
Poor response to timed, scheduled, pre-planned activities which interfere with immediacy of response
Tends to ignore structure
Self descriptions tend to point to essence (Hilliard 1976, pp. 36–38)

learning, or their experiences. In fact, they will probably be considered deviant and disruptive in the analytically oriented learning environment of the school (Cohen 1971).

Hilliard (1976) agrees that most schools support the analytic cognitive style, and contrasts these schools with those based on the relational cognitive style (Table 2.3).

Origins of cognitive style

Cohen (1971) suggests that children develop cognitive styles based upon the socialization they receive in their families and friendships. Children who live in structured families with "formal" styles of group organization have been observed to function with the analytical cognitive style. Those children who live in more fluid or "shared-function" primary groups, are more likely to exhibit the relational cognitive style.

Table 2.3. The school.

As it is in general *(analytical . . .)*	*As it could be* *(relational . . .)*
Rules	Freedom
Standardization	Variation
Conformity	Creativity
Memory for specific facts	Memory for essence
Regularity	Novelty
Rigid order	Flexibility
"Normality"	Uniqueness
Differences equal deficits	Sameness equals oppression
Preconceive	Improvise
Precision	Approximate
Logical	Psychological
Atomistic	Global
Egocentric	Sociocentric
Convergent	Divergent
Controlled	Expressive
Meanings are universal	Meanings are contextual
Direct	Indirect
Cognitive	Affective
Linear	Patterned
Mechanical	Humanistic
Unison	Individual in group
Hierarchical	Democratic
Isolation	Integration
Deductive	Inductive
Scheduled	Targets of opportunity
Thing focused	People focus
Constant	Evolving
Sign oriented	Meaning oriented
Duty	Loyalty (Hilliard 1976, p. 41)

Although that explanation has some merit, more work is needed to describe the socialization of Black children that leads to their distinctive cognitive styles.

Affective orientation

The cognitive styles of Black people seem to place a greater degree of emphasis upon affect than Anglo-Americans. Some scholars suggest that the emotion-charged, people-oriented quality of Black expression is a part of the African heritage.

> Knowledge in Western societies is largely derived from such propositions as "I think, therefore, I am." The non-Western heritage of Afro-Americans suggests that knowledge stems from the proposition that, "I feel, therefore I think, therefore, I am." (Dixon and Foster 1971, p. 18)

> The uniqueness of Black culture can be explained in that it is a culture whose emphasis is on the nonverbal . . . in Black culture, it is the experience that counts, not what is said. (Lester 1969, p. 87)

This does not mean that Black people do not think or conceptualize their experience symbolically. Intellectual analysis disconnected from feelings leads to incomplete knowledge of the world (Haskins and Butts 1973).

There are research studies (Gitter, Black, and Mostofsky 1972; Young 1970) that find Black children to be more feeling oriented, people oriented, and more proficient at nonverbal communication than White children. It is important to determine the implications of these attributes for their cognitive development (Gitter, Black, and Mostofsky 1972).

Young (1970) suggests that White children are object oriented and have numerous opportunities to manipulate objects and discover properties and relationships. Consequently, this society's educational system is very object oriented, and classrooms are filled with educational hardware and technology—books, listening stations, learning centers, televisions, programmed instruction, learning kits, and so forth.

In contrast, research with Black children finds them to be more people oriented. Most Black children grow up in large families where they have a great deal of human interaction. While traveling in Africa, I was interested in the kinds of dolls with which the children of Ghana play. One mother informed me that African children do not play with dolls, they play with their mother's babies!

This high degree of people orientation may account for the indifference with which some Black children regard books and other materials. It may also explain why some teachers complain that Black children will not work independently, but will cling to the teacher. I observed a classroom in which there were children who would work only when older children assisted them individually. This cultural trait should be acknowledged by providing more human interaction in the learning process.

Young (1970) provides evidence about childrearing practices that influence this people orientation:

> Even though household composition varies widely in the Black community, each is almost certain to contain many different types of people of all ages to hold and play with the baby. In many cases, the physical closeness between infants and adults is reinforced by the fact that they are often observed to sleep with their parents or either parent alone. There is a kind of rhythm found between eating and napping with short periods of each activity found with frequent repetition. This rhythm is very different from the disciplined long span of attention cultivated in middle-class childrearing and expected in schools. (p. 276)

Because Black babies are held so much of the time, there is an immediate response to urination and bowel movements. Hence, from an early age, there is an association in the infant's mind between these functions, and action from the mother. Consequently, when the mother seeks to toilet train the child (in the early and stringent manner that has been observed in the Black community), the child is accustomed to her direct involvement in this process. In contrast, the transition is more startling for middle-class American infants whose functions typically occur alone. The mother begins to interfere with bowel and bladder activity after many months of only cursory attention. There is greater continuity, then, in the behavior of Black mothers.

Young (1970) contrasts the highly personal interaction with the low object orientation found in Black families. She noticed that the few objects given to the babies were plastic toys that may have been picked up in the supermarket while shopping. Also, when babies reached to grasp an object or feel a surface, they were often redirected to feeling the holder's face or engaged in a game of rubbing faces as a substitute. This inhibition of exploration is possible because:

> there are always eyes on the baby and idle hands to take away the forbidden objects and then distract the frustrated baby. The personal is thus often substituted for the impersonal. (pp. 279–280)

This affective orientation may be a critical factor that is overlooked in traditional educational settings. Rapport with the teacher in educational settings and rapport with the examiner in testing settings seems to be strongly related to academic performance for Black students and not very critical for Whites. Zigler and his colleagues (Zigler and Butterfield 1968; Zigler, Abelson, and Seitz 1973) found that when a good rapport is established between an examiner during a standardized testing session, Black children exhibit significantly superior test performance than when it is not. Such a difference was not found in the White middle-class sample.

Piestrup (1973) identifies some factors which create good rapport in the teacher-Black student interaction, including warmth, verbal interplay during instruction, rhythmic style of speech, and distinctive intonation in speech patterns. When those factors are present, first-grade Black pupils show increased reading proficiency.

Contrasts between Nigerian and Western cultures

It may be useful to examine some aspects of African culture to identify antecedents of the affective orientation of Afro-Americans. Ebsen (1973) analyzes the childrearing practices found in Nigeria and points out differences in United States and African cultures. He refers to the clusters of African attitudes and modes of response as the "care syndrome." Most Africans grow up in a small rural community and are imbued from early childhood with an empathetic concern for others. In contrast, children who grow up in Western societies often do not know their neighbors, do not care about the people in their communities, and do not offer help to those who are in even desperate need.

Ebsen suggests that the African modes of childrearing give rise to the development of humane attitudes and the care syndrome. Unlike Western childrearing, African socialization emphasizes the closeness of people. Physical and psychological closeness is reinforced by encouragement of body contact between people. Most African children are breast fed for longer periods of time than in other societies. Before and after children learn to walk, they are held a great deal of the time by an older sibling. In most cases, infants sleep with their mothers until a new baby arrives. African children learn early in childhood to embrace relatives and friends in greeting them or thanking them for a special favor. Thus, the children grow up in a social network characterized by physical closeness, acceptance, and care. African children expect to receive affection and comfort and learn to give it when it is needed by others. By the time African children are six years old, they begin to take responsibility for providing care for a younger sibling. They carry the child on their backs, cradle the child on their laps, and learn to respond with body contact and carrying behavior to fit the needs of the child.

Ebsen believes that in Western society, objects come between children and their mothers. Babies are more prone to be bottle fed, pushed around in baby carriages, placed in playpens to play alone, and left in separate rooms in a different bed for sleeping. These gadgets come physically between babies and their mothers' bodies and interfere with the physical and psychological body warmth that is provided in Africa.

From the African viewpoint, Western children are socialized into a life of detachment and impersonalness. These early attitudes are also expressed later in the detached urban environment. People are seen as things in the distance or numbers in the computer. A basic aloofness toward people begins with the distance from the mother created by the feeding bottle and the baby carriage.

Ebsen suggests that the care syndrome is reflected in the use of language among African people. One key indicator is the system of elaborate and emotional greetings. Greetings always include inquiries about people who are important to the person, in contrast to Western greetings which discuss the weather and rarely inquire about human life and conditions.

> The closest they ever seem to come to some concern for the individual is with "How are you?" And even that in American usage has become impersonalized into a mere "Hi." (p. 208)

African languages seem to express caring and feeling to a greater extent than Western languages, too.

The extended family system also supports the care syndrome. Children see parents, grandparents, uncles, aunts, and cousins as a part of everyday life. The survival of the family depends upon how the members care about and provide for each other.

The nuclear family structure of father-mother-child in Western culture does not encourage this extended caring network. Grandparents usually must fend for themselves during their last years or be sent to retirement homes filled with strangers and impersonal relationships.

Brazelton, Young, and Bullowa (1971) support Ebsen's thesis in a study in which they compare infants born to Zambian mothers and infants born to White American mothers. The health of the Zambian mothers was not optimal, so the Zambian infants weighed less, were shorter, and less healthy than the White infants.

The two groups of infants were examined on days one, five, and ten after birth. On the day one examination, the Zambian infants scored significantly lower on following with eyes, motor activity, irritability, rapidity of buildup, and alertness. By day ten, however, the Zambian babies had surpassed the American infants in cuddliness, reactivity to stimulation, alertness, social interest, and consolability. The Zambian mothers' high-contact, loving environment for their babies provided more handling and feeding contact with their infants than the American mothers.

Nonverbal communication

Lower-class families have been reported to have a minimal amount of verbal exchange (Young 1970). Young states that this is because of the abundance of communication in other forms. She observes that people in these families look deeply into each other's eyes, not speaking, but seeming to communicate fully. Parents use this technique to impress a point on a child. Black people often avoid meeting the eyes of Whites, and this has been interpreted as a gesture of nonequality or nonattention. However, Young suggests that it may instead be a gesture of noncommunicativeness. The gaze of Whites is avoided to cut off that intense level of communication that Black people share with each other. Or, because it is a part of African heritage to respect elders, to look an authority figure directly in the eye is considered defiant and disrespectful.

Other forms of Black nonverbal communication are the mother's caressing of the baby, and children sitting in a circle rubbing bare feet. Young also noted what she calls a "mutuality" in family relations exhibited in remarks that pass between mothers and children.

"I'm tired," the three-year-old girl complains. "I'm tired too," her mother responds. "I want some ice cream," the eight-year-old

says wistfully as the ice cream truck passes. "I want some too,"
is the mother's way of saying no. This echoing of words and tone
of voice is a common speech pattern. One does not see mothers
and children clash and contend. (p. 296)

Two other studies (Newmeyer 1970; Gitter, Black, and Mostofsky 1972) support the hypothesis that Black culture develops
proficiency in nonverbal communication. Newmeyer had a
group of young Black and White males act out a number of
emotions nonverbally. The Black children were better at en-
acting the emotions so that others perceived them correctly.
Gitter, Black, and Mostofsky conducted a study with Black and
White college students. Each student was shown still photo-
graphs of professional actors attempting to portray each of
seven emotions. The Black students made significantly more
correct judgments of the emotions portrayed.

Physical development

Morgan (1976) suggests that Black infants are superior in all
aspects of development when the mothers have adequate pre-
natal care. He also points out that Black children are more active
and have more physical energy than White children.

Black lower-income mothers have been criticized for not providing enough toys for their children (Morgan 1976). Compensatory education programs often purchased toys and playthings
to distribute to these families. Morgan indicts such efforts.

> Little thought was given to the fact that the tinker toy concept
> dictates that children are expected to sit in the crib or thereabouts
> and play quietly with their toys until their favorite TV program
> comes on. Without these toys, of course, mother and child touch,
> exchange various forms of communications and learn from one
> another. (p. 133)

The Black child in school

Morgan (1976) maintains that the schools do not support the
natural energy level of Black children who need an active environment for successful learning. He states that this is particularly true of lower-income children whose parents emphasize survival skills rather than conformity, docility, and quiet
manners which are more typical of middle-class childrearing

where upward mobility is sought.

Black children enter school for the first time with excitement and enthusiasm. However, the school crushes the freedom and creativity of children who cannot channel their energy until given permission to release it. Consequently Black children elicit more punishment and are labeled hyperactive more frequently because of their high motoric activity (Morgan 1976).

Morgan (1976) believes that Black mothers often ignore their children's motoric precocity and do not seek to extend it because development in that area might interfere with the child's ability to be integrated into the school system of White low motor expectations. This situation, he maintains, is detrimental to the natural learning styles of Black children.

Morgan (1976) suggests that Black children need schools that are "uncrowded, open and airy with a great deal of natural light, [and] plenty of private space for teachers and learners" (p. 130). He also suggests that model classrooms should be established for research purposes where "special nonpunitive environments are created as centers of learning for children who require more free space and movement than what schools normally allow" (p. 130).

Boykin (1978) suggests that the Black home environment provides an abundance of stimulation, intensity, and variation through high noise levels and large numbers of people. This has been analyzed as "over stimulation" and as creating "conceptual deafness" by some social scientists (Marans and Lourie 1967; Goldman and Sanders 1969; Wachs, Uzgiris, and Hunt 1971). However, Boykin hypothesizes that this stimulating home environment produces greater psychological and behavioral verve in Black children than children from a White middle-class setting.

Black children may learn faster with techniques that incorporate body movement into the learning process. Guttentag (1972) and Guttentag and Ross (1972) found that Black preschool children possess a greater movement repertoire than both lower- and middle-class White preschoolers. They also showed that Black children learn simple verbal concepts easier when they utilize movement than when they are taught by a more traditional format. Massari, Hayweiser, and Meyer (1969) also found that the children who could inhibit movement have higher IQ scores.

Boykin (1977) found that varying the format in problem-solving tasks presented to Black and White children does not make a difference in the performance of the White children. However, Black children perform markedly better with the varied format.

Thus, especially for Black children, schools are rather unstimulating and monotonous places to be (Silberman 1970; Holt 1964). Boykin suggests that the reason White children are more successful at academic tasks than Black children is that they have a greater tolerance for monotony. Perhaps Black children are not as successful in school because they are relatively more intolerant of monotonous, boring tasks, and the sterile unstimulating school environment.

The effectiveness of the use of rhythm in speech and verbal interplay by teachers of Black children may also connect culturally with Black children who interact rhythmically with their mothers at home. Young (1970) observed a "contest" style of speech between Black mothers and children in which they volley rhythmically and the child is encouraged to be assertive and to develop an individual style. Young suggests there is a distinctive manner by which Black mothers give directions for household tasks that approximates the call and response patterns found in Black music. (A mother's communication of directions for household tasks uses few words, and tasks for which she has to give instructions are broken down into small units with brief directions for each short task following completion of the previous one.)

Boykin (1977) concludes that affective stimulation and vervistic stimulation are necessary for the Black child to be motivated to achieve in an academic setting. He suggests that this is the reason why Black children become turned off by the sterile, boring school environment and seek other arenas for achievement and expression. He suggests that "perhaps we can facilitate the academic/task performance of the Black child if we increase the 'soulfulness' of the academic task setting" (p. 21).

Looking toward the future

What do we need to know about Black culture in order to design learning environments for Black children? We must conduct a wide-ranging examination of all aspects of at-home interaction that can provide descriptive information about the world view of the Black child. These areas especially deserve attention from Black researchers who wish to lead the work that defines their own culture and learning styles.

Movement: An examination of the amount and utilization of space that is occupied during children's play is needed. It would be interesting to determine the amount of time Black children spend in quiet activities as compared with active movement, because this would have implications for the length of time adults should require children to sit and concentrate on tasks.

Dance: How much reinforcement are Black children given as toddlers to dance in addition to encouragement to walk? Could early expressions of rhythm through dance have any influence upon the physical precocity of Black children? Does early proficiency in dance affect mathematical ability?

Music: What are the stages by which Black children respond to music? How prevalent is music in the Black environment? What is the preferred type of music? How often are songs sung to children and by children? What songs are sung? Why are Black children remarkably able to memorize popular songs? How can that ability be transferred to other types of learnings?

Home environment: Any description of environments in which Black children live, play, and develop should encompass artistic descriptors as well as indicators of affluence and educational enrichment. Note should be taken of color preferences in Black homes as well as any other distinctive features in decor, furniture styles, and arrangement. This information may be useful in designing learning environments for Black children. For example, Black children may learn most effectively or exhibit distinctive moods based upon the colors of the classroom walls.

Fashion: Black people have emphasized personal distinctiveness in their dress, and Black males in particular have influenced the fashion industry by setting trends such as wide-leg pants and bright colors in suits and shirts. A study of the type of clothing worn by Black children for various occasions might reveal the extent to which children are dressed according to the tastes of their parents, and at what age the children begin to express preferences and make choices. Those choices could be analyzed to determine how much influence the Black cultural milieu has on Black children's dress.

Folklore: An ethnographic study of expressive styles should record the folklore of Black children. Most studies of the language of Black children have been from a linguistic perspective, but it may also be useful to study the verbal skills of Black children. There are also stylistic dimensions of the oral tradition in Black culture as described by Silberman (1970): call and response, rhythmic patterns, spontaneity, and concreteness. Games, stories, chants, jump rope rhymes, curse words, and "playin' the dozens" could be analyzed to ascertain the psychological processes they reflect. It is also important to understand the way in which the culture of the Black community affects the fantasy of Black children.

Nutrition: A study of Black children's nutrition may be important in interpreting their behavior. Any study of foods popular with Blacks should encompass food selection and spicing. This information has obvious implications for health services. It would also be helpful in planning menus and nutrition education programs for Black children.

Rookwood (1978) suggests investigating the mealtime patterns of Black families. Teachers are often encouraged to serve meals family style. Rookwood observed a teacher in a Head Start center who had the children eat one by one. When questioned about the practice, the teacher replied that this pattern of eating was more similar to the style of eating of many of the children at home wherein family members "catch a plate" whenever they arrive and are hungry. She found that the children play less at the table, eat more, and seem to feel better. The teacher stated that children eat better when they can concentrate on eating rather than telling the teacher the color of the peas.

Magical-spiritual beliefs: Rubin (1975) notes a deep concern with the spiritual and the supernatural among Black children. Examining these modes will help to better understand the world view of the Black child and determine the implications for concept development.

                              *   *   *   *   *

The story has been told of a child named Akin who was accustomed to hearing bedtime stories each night that told of Tarzan and the Lion. In each episode, Tarzan always defeated the Lion. So, one night, Akin asked his mother when the Lion was going to win. His mother closed the book and sighed, "Honey, I guess the Lion will beat Tarzan when lions begin to write books."

References

Akbar, N. Paper presented at the Annual Meeting of the National Black Child Development Institute, San Francisco, California, 1975.

Boykin, A. W. "Experimental Psychology from a Black Perspective: Issues and Examples." In *Final Report from the Third Conference on Empirical Research in Black Psychology*, ed. W. Cross. Washington, D.C.: National Institute of Education, 1977.

Boykin, A. W. "Psychological/Behavioral Verve in Academic/Task Performance: Three Theoretical Considerations." *Journal of Negro Education* 47 (1978): 343–354.

Brazelton, T. B.; Young, G. G.; and Bullowa, M. "Inception and Resolution of Early Developmental Pathology: A Case History." *Journal of the American Academy of Child Psychiatry* 10, no. 1 (January 1971): 124–135.

Cohen, R. "The Influence of Conceptual Rule-Sets on Measures of Learning Ability." In *Race and Intelligence*. Washington, D.C.: American Anthropological Association, 1971.

Dixon, V. J., and Foster, B. G. *Beyond Black or White*. Boston: Little, Brown, 1971.

DuBois, W. E. B. "Of Our Spiritual Strivings." In *The Souls of Black Folk*. New York: New American Library, 1903.

Ebsen, A. "The Care Syndrome: A Resource for Counseling in Africa." *Journal of Negro Education* 42, no. 2 (Spring 1973): 205–211.

Gitter, A. G.; Black, G. H.; and Mostofsky, D. I. "Race and Sex in Perception of Emotion." *Journal of Social Issues* 28 (1972): 63–78.

Goldman, R., and Sanders, J. "Cultural Factors and Hearing." *Exceptional Children* 35 (1969): 489–490.

Guttentag, M. "Negro-White Differences in Children's Movement." *Perceptual and Motor Skills* 35 (1972): 435–436.

Guttentag, M., and Ross, S. "Movement Responses in Simple Concept Learning." *American Journal of Orthopsychiatry* 42 (1972): 657–665.

Haskins, J., and Butts, H. F. *The Psychology of Black Language*. New York: Barnes & Noble, 1973.

Hilliard, A. "Alternatives to IQ Testing: An Approach to the Identification of Gifted Minority Children." Final report to the California State Department of Education, 1976.

Holt, J. *How Children Fail*. New York: Dell, 1964.

Lester, J. *Look Out Whitey! Black Power's Gon' Get Your Mama!* New York: Grove, 1969.

Marans, A., and Lourie, R. "Hypotheses Regarding the Effects of Child-

95086

LIBRARY
COLBY-SAWYER COLLEGE
NEW LONDON, N.H. 03257

rearing Patterns on the Disadvantaged Child." In *The Disadvantaged Child*, ed. J. Hellmuth. Seattle, Wash.: Special Child Publications, 1967.

Massari, D.; Hayweiser, L.; and Meyer, J. "Activity Level and Intellectual Functioning in Deprived Preschool Children." *Developmental Psychology* 1 (1969): 286–290.

Morgan, H. "Neonatal Precocity and the Black Experience." *Negro Educational Review* 27 (April 1976): 129–134.

Newmeyer, J. A. "Creativity and Nonverbal Communication in Preadolescent White and Black Children." Unpublished doctoral dissertation, Harvard University, 1970.

Piestrup, A. *Black Dialect Interference and Accommodation of Reading Instruction in First Grade*. Monograph #4. Berkeley, Calif.: University of California, Language Behavior Research Laboratory, 1973.

Rookwood, J. Personal communication, 1978.

Rubin, M. Personal communication, 1975.

Silberman, C. *Crisis in the Classroom*. New York: Random House, 1970.

Wachs, T.; Uzgiris, I.; and Hunt, J. McV. "Cognitive Development in Infants of Different Age Levels and from Different Environmental Backgrounds: An Explanatory Investigation." *Merrill-Palmer Quarterly* 17 (1971): 283–316.

Young, V. H. "Family and Childhood in a Southern Georgia Community." *American Anthropologist* 72 (1970): 269–288.

Zigler, E.; Abelson, W.; and Seitz, V. "Motivational Factors in the Performance of Economically Disadvantaged Children on the Peabody Picture Vocabulary Test." *Child Development* 44, no. 2 (June 1973): 294–303.

Zigler, E., and Butterfield, E. "Motivational Aspects of Changes in IQ Test Performance of Culturally Deprived Nursery School Children." *Child Development* 39, no. 1 (1968): 1–14.

Revised from an earlier version that appeared in *Young Children* 36, no. 2 (January 1981): 37–50. © 1981 by the National Association for the Education of Young Children, 1834 Connecticut Ave., N.W., Washington, DC 20009.

Terry Tafoya

3
Coyote in the Classroom:
The Use of American-Indian Oral Tradition with Young Children

Ana Chush Iwacha
Son'Ahchi
Once Upon a Time

 ach one of these phrases opens expectations for a particular culture. They are part of a ritual for the Sahaptin-, Zuni-, and English-speaking peoples. In terms of oral traditions, all three phrases refer to a time that is not now. The significance of this time distinction will be discussed later.

The stories these words introduce are what the Zuni people call *telapnaawe*, stories that in English, we might call *fiction*. There are other terms that introduce stories believed to be true—historical accounts. To understand this, consider how the phrase, "In the news tonight . . ." puts you in the mood to hear Dan Rather describe an increase in energy costs.

English is a difficult language to use in conveying certain concepts. Take, for example, the connotations of the words *legend, myth, fairy tale, story.* All imply something that is not true—something out of contact with reality. What the non-Indian community needs to understand is that these stories may more fully describe reality than any newscast, especially in relation to young children.

Young children do not perceive the world as adults do. As Wartella (1979) states:

Adult perceptions of children have changed radically since the court of Louis XIV when children were dressed and regarded as miniature adults. Anyone who has observed a five-year-old and his 10-year-old sibling talking while watching television can intuitively recognize that children think differently and communicate differently. The "adjustment" of most adults in the way we talk to children reflects our strong intuition that they are not miniature adults. (p. 7)

What is the earliest memory you have? How old were you? You simply don't recall much from your early childhood because you thought differently in those days from the way you do now. Your earliest memories were encoded in a manner so different you no longer have access to them, except for an occasional, powerful moment usually associated with something emotional.

In working with traditional oral stories, we are dealing with words heard by generations of children, and adults. Imagine, if you will, a pebble worn smooth by its interaction with a stream. A traditional story is like that—washed by the stream of time until what is not essential to it has been washed away. To become part of the rich oral tradition of a Native culture, the story has to speak to children in a language they understand . . . and there is a child in all of us.

Bettelheim (1976), in his book, *The Uses of Enchantment*, relates:

> For a story truly to hold the child's attention, it must entertain him and arouse his curiosity. But to enrich his life, it must stimulate his imagination; help him to develop his intellect and to clarify his emotions; be attuned to his anxieties and aspirations; give full recognition to his difficulties, while at the same time suggesting solutions to the problems which perturb him. In short, it must at one and the same time relate to all aspects of his personality—and this without ever belittling, but, on the contrary, giving full credence to the seriousness of the child's predicaments, while simultaneously promoting confidence in himself and in his future. (p. 5)

Bettelheim is not addressing the nature of an Indian child, but the psychological needs of all human children, as shown, for example, in the enormous acceptance of the movie *Star Wars*. In the United States, the Native-American population has perhaps maintained its oral tradition and kept its stories alive better than most groups. The descendants of Europeans have fossilized their own oral traditions in the form of written fairy tales.

At the risk of belaboring my point, I must repeat that the term *fairy tale* is not a satisfactory translation of Native-American oral traditions. Not all Native-American oral traditions are properly classified as fiction. Indeed, all Native-American languages I am familiar with make a strong distinction between those stories created to educate and enlighten and those stories repeated for their historical significance. Let's look closely at a particular story from the Pacific Northwest in light of its meaning to children. It is often difficult to trace the origin of any one story. Through trade, intermarriage, gift, happenstance, or even theft, stories are passed down. Traditionally stories are possessions just as your car or your clothes are possessions, and not everyone had or has the right to tell them. This legend is from the Yakima Indians of eastern Washington state. I've adapted it for use on a flannel board with young children. In using this story, I have never lost the attention of my audience. I include it in this particular form as a curriculum piece you can try in your own classroom. While traditionally we never used flannel boards in storytelling, some Native-American cultures have used devices, for example, story knives which are knives used by certain Eskimo groups as a doodling device while telling a story. (The scribblings left on the snow or mud correspond to the actions of the story, but would be impossible to decipher without hearing the actual story. Other props used to heighten the dramatic impact of a story include masks or unusual clothing.) The original legend is, of course, much longer but involves certain cultural elements that would have to be explained to non-Yakima, and even urban Yakima, children, so I have attempted to retain its most important elements in my adaptation.

When Mosquitoes Ate People
From the Yakima Indians

Needed for flannel board story:
One set of legs
Breechcloth
Moccasins
One skinny mosquito man torso with long sharp nose
One torso with stomach bulge
One torso with large stomach

One torso with huge stomach
One torso with enormous stomach
One door frame in green with serrated edges to show thorns
One coyote
Assorted animal people

*As the story is told, the appropriate torso is placed on the set
of legs. I usually go through the legend once and then ask
the children to tell the legend to me to check on their understanding. (I recall telling a legend about the ant fasting, because fasting is a form of prayer for some tribes. Imagine my
chagrin when I heard a seven-year-old calmly relate that the
ant prayed fast!) Using the flannel board also allows young
children to develop their manipulation skills. (I recall using
this story with a reservation Head Start program and seeing
the sense of accomplishment of a child with Down syndrome
as he took his turn in adjusting the flannel figures while the
children were retelling the legend.)*

Narrator:	Long time ago there was a terrible monster called the Mosquito Man. He was a giant who had a big nose that he used to spear people and suck out their blood. All the people were afraid of him.
Mosquito Man:	Blood soup . . . I'm hungry for blood soup.
Animals:	What should we do? The Mosquito Man will eat us! Someone save us!
Narrator:	Coyote heard the people and decided to help them.
Coyote:	To save you we must ask the help of the plant people. All of the plant people with thorns . . . the thistles, the wild roses, the black-berries, will you help protect us from the Mosquito Monster?
Plants:	We will help you.
Narrator:	And so the people gathered branches and thorns from all the plant people. They hung them around the door in the long house where the different people lived.
Coyote:	Now we must call the Mosquito Man to us.
Mosquito Man:	Blood soup . . . I want some blood soup.
Animals:	Mosquito Man, Mosquito Man . . . come have dinner with us. We invite you to a feast. We'll have blood soup.

Mosquito Man: A feast? A feast?

Animals: Come with us.

Mosquito Man: What a strange door you have on your long house!

Coyote: It is very beautiful with roses and berries and thistles, isn't it?

Mosquito Man: I'm hungry.

Animals: Here's some blood soup. Eat all you want.

Narrator: Then the Mosquito Man ate all the blood soup in the huge bowl he had been given.

Mosquito Man: Delicious soup. Wonderful soup.

Animals: There's more. Have some more.

Narrator: The animal people brought out more blood soup. The Mosquito Man ate and ate. Soon his tummy began to stick out.

Mosquito Man: Delicious soup. Wonderful soup.

Animals: What a wonderful appetite you have to be so hungry. Have some more blood soup.

Narrator: The Mosquito man continued to eat. More and more blood soup was brought out by the animal people. Even as they watched, the Mosquito Man's tummy began to grow and grow.

Mosquito Man: Delicious soup. Wonderful soup.

Animals: More! Have some more blood soup!

Narrator: Bigger and bigger the monster's tummy became. Still the animal people brought out more soup for him.

Mosquito Man: Delicious soup! Wonderful soup! More! More!

Narrator: Finally the animal people knew it was time.

Coyote: Now everyone! Everyone run from the Mosquito Man!

Mosquito Man: Where are you going? You can't get away from me. I'll catch you and make you into more blood soup!

Narrator: Coyote and the other people ran as fast as they could out the door. The Mosquito Monster came after them, but he was now so fat he could no longer run.

Mosquito Man: I'll get you. You can't get away from me!

Narrator: But the Mosquito Man was so fat now he couldn't fit through the door anymore. His

fat tummy hit the sharp thorns of the door
and he exploded. He burst apart into the little
mosquitoes we still have today. The mosquitoes can't kill you anymore, but they can
sure make you itch!

                *   *   *   *   *

Why do children (and adults) enjoy this legend so much?
Remember that a legend is retold within the Indian community
year after year. It is not simplified (as I have simplified this
story for the flannel board) for a child's sake. Until the bow-
dlerizing by Christian missionaries, legends were not cleaned
up by eliminating references of a sexual or bodily nature.
Rather, the audience changed while the story remained the
same. A young child could simply not fully understand the
sexual elements. As the audience matured, their perceptions
of the story altered and expanded revealing new levels of meaning.

For the young child, the story of the Mosquito Man is an
exciting one, but it speaks to children in a very fundamental
way. The Mosquito Man is a giant. What are adults in size
relation to a child?

Relating a case history, Bettelheim (1976) tells of a mother
who read to her five-year-old child the story of "Jack and the
Beanstalk":

> His response at the end of the story was, "There aren't any such
> things as giants, are there?" Before the mother could give her son
> the reassuring reply which was on her tongue—and which would
> have destroyed the value of the story for him—he continued, "but
> there are such things as grown-ups, and they're like giants." At
> the ripe old age of five, he understood the encouraging message
> of the story: although adults can be experienced as frightening
> giants, a little boy with cunning can get the better of them. (p.
> 27)

In relation to the size of the Mosquito giant, Coyote is small
but his cunning allows him to defeat the monster. It is significant, too, how the Mosquito Man is defeated—not killed, but
transformed from a deadly, invincible enemy to a tiny annoy-
ance that the smallest human child can overcome with a single
handslap. This story holds a child's attention by, as mentioned
earlier in Bettelheim's description, "giving full credence to the
seriousness of the child's predicaments, while simultaneously
promoting confidence in himself and in his future" (p. 5).

Certain symbolism can be read into the blood soup (the animal people contribute something of themselves to continue their own lives) but one must realize that, from a cultural standpoint, blood soup is a nutritious culinary delight for numerous tribes. More important is the involvement of the plants in defeating the monster. The people cannot overcome the giant by themselves—it is only when they manage to create unity with another part of nature that they can achieve their purpose.

This concept of the unity of various elements is an essential part of Native-American tradition. Many of the stories deal with seeing through the eyes of different animals, and in so doing, achieving altered perceptions that serve to round out one's personality. A person who constantly stays fixed in one mode of perception is incomplete and is unable to function to her or his full capacity. Life itself is not fixed in one mode. These animal eyes are metaphysical representations that require use of the right side of the brain. This point should be a special consideration for research in cerebral dominance theory. Thus, we are not working with simple children's stories, but a culture's method of providing enlightenment to a part of the individual seldom approached by conventional non-Indian education.

We can therefore see that a legend like the Mosquito Monster touches the child's self-perception and the child's relationship with the world. For the young child, the world is a dangerous place. In the story, death in the form of the monster is a natural part of the world, just as in the everyday world fast automobiles, stairs, and scalding water, for example, are constant threats. The story teaches that threats can be handled—not quickly, not easily, but with proper actions and patience.

As I mentioned before, by placing the story in an earlier time, we remove the problem of confusing actuality of the everyday with the actions taking place in the legend. This safeguard does not exist with the excessively realistic stories that have been in vogue for children for the last two generations. The contemporary American-Indian child does not have to worry about being attacked by a Mosquito Monster. However, after watching a movie about earthquakes, infernos, or floods, a child might walk out into daylight, see the same buildings, pavement, and automobiles that were just destroyed, and have good reason for being afraid.

In examining this simplified legend, we are confining ourselves to only a small part of its original meaning. Imagine describing a rainbow by confining yourself to talking about yellow. But by analyzing legends from a psychological and educational standpoint, administrators feel better about using them in the classroom. Suddenly they aren't simply children's stories, but curriculum materials.

Traditionally for Native Americans, the manner of storytelling—its timing as well as its content—also instills certain cultural values and concepts for which there are no equivalents in English. Stories are told when the time is appropriate and not because 11:30 a.m. is circle time. Stories are constantly referred to in order to illustrate points children should remember or to modify their behavior. Traditionally stories were told in a cycle so that many, many different stories were heard during the seasons (winter is almost universally the proper storytelling time for Native-American people). This is beneficial because each child's emotional development is different. One child may need a parent-centered story to better understand the home situation, while another more independent child may benefit from a legend dealing with a character involved with leaving home to seek her or his destiny.

Finally, one must understand what storytelling is all about. It is a ceremony in itself. American-Indian people have long understood the power of words and images. True storytellers reaffirm and recreate reality in their actions. Storytellers give part of themselves to their audience. Most teachers lose this understanding of their students when they lecture. When you read from a book, the book speaks to the child. They aren't your words and the child knows it. When you show a film, its images aren't yours and they aren't those of the child. Children's imaginations are not challenged into growing unless they picture what characters look like, how they move, how they dress.

I urge you . . . tell a story. Experience it. American Indians have no monopoly on oral traditions. Look to your own heritage and memorize one of your own people's stories to share with children and give them that part of yourself that grows by sharing.

There are also many fine anthologies of American-Indian legends available that all children will enjoy. I suggest you look to those that are tribally initiated or approved, such as *The Indian Reading Series: Stories and Legends of the Northwest, Grandfather Stories of the Navahos,* or *We-Gyet Wanders On.*

You will also benefit from those stories collected by American Indians like George Clutesi in his *Son of Raven, Son of Deer*, or *Wo Ya-Ka Pi*, by Gilbert Walking Bull. However, our stories were never created for a printed page; ink robs them of the songs, gestures, and intonations that are so much a part of them. But allow Coyote into the classroom. He's sly. He may never leave.

References

Bettelheim, B. *The Uses of Enchantment: The Meaning and Importance of Fairy Tales*. New York: Knopf, 1976.

Wartella, E., ed. *Children Communicating: Media and Development of Thought, Speech, Understanding*. Sage Annual Review of Communications Research, Vol. 7. Beverly Hills, Calif.: Sage, 1979.

Suggested story books

The Book Builders of 'KSAN. *We-Gyet Wanders On: Legends of the Northwest*. Seattle, Wash.: Hancock House, 1977. This is a beautiful book printed in a bilingual edition of English and the Gitksan language. It chronicles the journeying of their ravenlike trickster character and is illustrated with superb northwest coastal art from the Kitanmax School of the Northwest Coast Indian Art in Hazelton, British Columbia.

Callaway, M., and Witherspoon, G., eds. *Grandfather Stories of the Navahos*. Phoenix, Ariz.: Navajo Curriculum Center Press, 1974. This is one of several texts developed by the Navajo Curriculum Center. Like the others, it features an English version of the legends suitable for use with young children, and illustrated by Native artists.

Clutesi, G. *Son of Raven, Son of Deer: Fables of the Tse-shaht People*. Sidney, British Columbia: Grey's Publishing, 1975. In addition to being an excellent collection of Northwest Coastal legends, this book also has an introduction that contrasts Native children's stories with European nursery rhymes, and suggests some essentials of traditional Indian education. The illustrations are by the artist.

The Indian Reading Series: Stories and Legends of the Northwest. Northwest Regional Educational Laboratory, 300 SW Sixth Ave., Portland, Ore. 97204. This is a most useful collaborative effort of several tribal representatives of the Pacific Northwest through a grant from the National Institute of Education. Intended as a supplemental reader series, these books (now available from first to fifth grade reading levels) are for the most part traditional Native-American legends that have been rewritten with the assistance of professional educators and the tribal members. There are also two sets of *Teacher's Manuals-Student Activity Cards* tied to the series that give teachers suggestions of expanded activities developed by Native-American consultants. For example, a class can be set up in *clan* systems. Each clan is represented by a different animal, and each animal represents different attributes that the students seek to achieve such as courage, patience, or cooperation. The student activity cards are used by the children themselves, and include questions that explore more subtle teachings of the stories, as well as provide individual activities to balance out the group activities provided by the teacher manual.

Tedlock, D., trans. *Finding the Center: Narrative Poetry of the Zuni Indians.* Lincoln, Neb.: University of Nebraska Press, 1972. This most interesting book is one of the few works that attempts to give the reader a feeling of narrative qualities of the translated stories of Andrew Peynetsa and Walter Sanchez by providing detailed guides to reading aloud.

Walking Bull, G. *Wo Ya-Ka Pi: Telling Stories of the Past and Present by American Indians.* Dallas, Ore.: Itemizer-Observer Press, 1976. Gilbert Walking Bull is a descendant of Sitting Bull and Crazy Horse. He is an Oglala Sioux from the Pine Ridge Reservation in South Dakota. These stories include translations of stories he heard as a child.

Margie K. Kitano

4

Early Education for Asian-American Children

The 1980 United States Census (Preliminary 1980 Census Results 1982) reveals that people of Asian and Pacific Island descent constitute a significant minority. In 1980, individuals of Chinese, Filipino, Japanese, Korean, Vietnamese, Hawaiian, and Samoan ancestry together numbered more than 3 million, at least double the population figure indicated by the 1970 Census.

Despite the large population of Asian Americans, little is known about specific educational needs, particularly at the early childhood and elementary levels. One factor that may underlie the sparsity of relevant educational literature is the stereotype of Asian Americans as members of a successful "model minority," a picture that may generalize to early school performance. In light of evidence contradicting the success image for income, mental health, and education (Sue, Sue, and Sue 1975), instructional practices more appropriate to the needs of Asian-American children must be identified.

Literature review

Even a cursory glance at literature pertinent to Asian-American early education reveals three facts. First, very little information is available on this topic, particularly with reference to the critical variables of learning style and orientation toward school. Second, some of the available empirical works are dated, use select samples, and/or fail to report information vital to the studies' replicability and credibility. Hence, only limited generalizations can be made to current educational practices. Third, Asian-American children's learning characteristics cannot be described without consideration of cultural variables, including culture-specific childrearing practices. The review is organized by subgroup, as each represents a unique culture. Order of presentation reflects population size. Unless otherwise noted, population statistics are extracted from "Preliminary 1980 Census Results" (1982).

Chinese

The Chinese, numbering 806,027 in 1980, have replaced the Japanese as the largest Asian-American subgroup. More than half of the Chinese population lives in the western states, 40 percent in California alone. Another quarter (27 percent) resides in the Northeast.

Cultural factors. Sue and Kirk (1972) suggest that family emphasis on tradition, conformity, respect for authority, and submergence of individuality fosters greater anxiety and less tolerance for ambiguity. Emphasis on family loyalty, control of behavior through guilt and shame, and distrust of outsiders contributes to the seeming absence of concern for social welfare. An investigation of Chinese-Americans and immigrants in Hawaii indicates that despite trends toward assimilation, traditional values and family systems persist (Young 1972). No one pattern characterizes all Chinese Americans, however, and the range of differences within the group requires consideration.

Several investigators (Borke and Sue 1972; Kriger and Kroes 1972; Steward and Steward 1973) attempt to define specific childrearing factors that affect Chinese-American children's behavior. In a study most relevant to the behavior of young children, Steward and Steward (1973) observed Anglo-, Mexican-, and Chinese-American mothers teaching their three-year-old children a sorting and motor skill game. Chinese-American mothers were less likely to initiate and complete teaching-learning "loops" which consisted of gaining the child's attention, providing instruction, waiting for the child's response, and providing feedback. Within this group, English-speaking Chinese mothers provided significantly more loops than did Chinese-speaking mothers. Chinese-American mothers also less frequently increased their specificity of instructions following children's requests for help. With regard to attitudes, Chinese-American mothers considered teaching to be an important part of the maternal role and had regular formal instruction for their preschool age children. It was noted that kindergarten teachers found that Chinese-American mothers often requested notification if the child did not learn.

Learning characteristics. Data from early studies investigating the tested intelligence of Chinese-American children suggest that no striking differences exist between Chinese- and Anglo-American children (Yeung 1921) and that both groups may demonstrate higher test performance than their Hawaiian, Japanese-, Filipino-, and Korean-American peers (Livesay 1942). Other investigators working in the 1920s reported higher scores on nonverbal than verbal measures of intelligence (Symonds 1924b) and equal or superior performance to Anglo-American children on tests that minimize language factors (Graham 1926). It was also reported that Chinese language school attendance had a negligible effect on acquisition and use of English in elementary school children (Symonds 1924a). Consistent with earlier findings, studies done in the 1960s (e.g., Stodolsky and Lesser 1967) indicate that Chinese-American boys and girls perform higher on spatial, numerical, and reasoning than verbal tasks. A more recent but methodologically limited study (Chen and Goon 1976) was interpreted as indicating that gifted, low-income, Asian-American children possessed verbal skills equal or superior to those of their non-Asian gifted peers despite the fact that English was their second language. An investigation of Chinese-American children attending a private school also failed to demonstrate a relationship between exposure to English and intelligence test scores (Yee and LaForge 1974). The authors suggest, as one explanation, that parents' positive attitudes toward learning and emphases on biculturalism, bilingualism, and English may mask potential differences. Although the effects of Chinese-English bilingualism on intelligence test performance remain unclear, bilingualism may affect learning in other ways. For example, bilingualism may impair fluency and flexibility on creativity measures, due to competing associations arising from the use of two different languages (Torrance et al. 1970).

Filipinos

With increased immigration since 1970, Filipino Americans

constitute the second largest Asian-American subgroup. The 1980 Census reports their population in the United States at 774, 640. Almost 70 percent of Filipino Americans live in the western states.

Cultural factors and learning characteristics. A few authors (e.g., Guthrie 1961) have attempted to describe aspects of Filipino culture regarding childrearing practices and values and their effect on behavior. Because the Filipino people come from many tribal and racial origins, reflecting cultural and language diversity, it is difficult to present a general discussion of childrearing patterns. Research has been done on intelligence test performance (Livesay 1942) and achievement motivation (Aldaba-Lim and Javillonar 1968; Kubany, Gallimore, and Buell 1970; Sloggett, Gallimore, and Kubany 1970) of Filipinos, but is limited to high school students.

Japanese

Japanese Americans now rank third in numbers of Asian-Americans, with a population size of 700, 747. The vast majority (80 percent) resides in the western states, primarily California and Hawaii.

Cultural factors. Two general features of Japanese-American culture have been identified as influencing psychological development: cultural values and family structure. Japanese and Chinese cultural values emphasize obedience, dependence on the family, formality in interpersonal relationships, and restraint in expressing emotion (Sue 1973). Consistent with these values, the Japanese family is structured to inhibit internal conflict and to foster extended dependency (Kitano 1973). The lines of authority are vertical, with the father in supreme position. Family members have well-defined roles and follow established ways of interacting with those in higher and lower positions of power. Each member is expected to mask strong feelings that may disrupt family harmony. The personality characteristics of Japanese-American students reflect these cultural values and family structures. Generalization of such traits to all Japanese Americans should be tempered, however, by findings of significant variation within the Japanese-American group.

Consistent with cultural values and family structure, Japanese childrearing practices have been described as involving less direct confrontation than American techniques, low verbosity but high control, provision of outside stimuli, diversion of the child's attention, and shaping of cooperation by reference to its effects on others. Parents control children's behavior by evoking fear of personal ridicule and shame on the family as primary sanctions and by appealing to obligation and duty (Kitano 1974).

A series of studies on maternal care and infant behavior in Japanese, Japanese-American, and Anglo-American families relates specific maternal behaviors to children's development (Caudill 1971; Caudill and Weinstein 1969). Results indicate that Anglo-American mothers engaged in more lively chatting to their infants, resulting in a higher level of infant vocalization and exploratory activity. Japanese mothers were observed to do more vocal lulling and rocking, fostering more physically passive infants. Comparable data obtained on third generation Japanese-American mothers (Sansei) and their infants indicate patterns closer to those of Anglo Americans than to those of the Japanese (Caudill and Frost 1972).

Other data on a small sample of Japanese-American mother-child pairs, however, suggest that Japanese-American mothers provide less training in verbal interaction than do Anglo-American mothers, resulting in lower child verbalization rates (Moritsugu 1971).

Learning characteristics. Little empirical work has been done to provide an adequate description of Japanese-American children's learning characteristics. Minor attention has been given to achievement, motivation, and cognitive style, but most has been directed at secondary level children. An early study comparing Anglo-American and Japanese-American children in California suggests that Japanese-American children were "inferior" to the former in mental processes involving memory and abstract thinking (Darsie 1926). The data indicate, however, that the Anglo-American children's superiority was generally limited to specifically linguistic tests; Japanese-American children were equal or superior on tests using concrete, nonverbal, visually-presented stimuli.

Only one study (Ayabe and Santo 1972) was found on cognitive styles. Japanese and Chinese second graders were compared with Hawaiian, Filipino-, and Samoan-American elementary school children in Hawaii on conceptual tempo, or speed of response. Results indicate that Chinese- and Japanese-American children with fast conceptual tempo produced

significantly fewer errors than fast tempo children of other
ethnicities. The authors suggest that Japanese and Chinese
cultural values of perseverance, restraint, and patience may
have led to greater accuracy in performance.

Koreans

The 1980 Census reported a Korean population in the United
States of 354,529, up 400 percent since 1970. Korean Americans
appear to be more dispersed in America than the Japanese and
Chinese subgroups. In 1980, 43 percent were living in the West,
19 percent in the Northeast, 18 percent in the north-central
states, and 20 percent in the South.

Cultural factors and learning characteristics. Perhaps due to
the relatively small number of Korean children in the United
States, a review of literature yields little empirical information
on their learning characteristics and the effect of their cultural
background on psychological development. However, the
unique problems faced by Korean-American children and the
effects on their schooling have been described (Hahn and Dobb
1975). Few educational programs designed specifically for Korean-American children exist, due perhaps to their small and
scattered numbers. Staggered immigration is characteristic of
Korean-American families, with one member arriving first, get-
ting settled, and sending for the others. This system often results in long periods of separation and large discrepancies between individual members in English fluency. In the schools,
Korean-American children encounter little exposure to their
own culture and are frequently mistaken for Chinese and Japanese. Korean cultural values with respect to education have
been described as including respect for the teacher, expectation
for a formal student-teacher relationship, and grade consciousness (Pitler 1977).

One effect of this relative isolation from cultural peers may
be lowered self-concept. In a comparison of Korean-American
and Black children on self-concept (Chang 1975), Korean Americans scored higher on items related to behavior, intelligence,
school status, happiness, and satisfaction. They were significantly lower, however, on physical appearance and popularity.
Chang attributes the lower scores on appearance and popularity
items to their isolation from other Korean children and con-
sequent feelings that they are physically different. Parents' positive attitudes toward school and childrearing practices are hy-

pothesized to account for Korean-American children's higher school-related self-concept scores relative to those of Black children.

Vietnamese

After the fall of Saigon in the spring of 1975, more than 130,000 Vietnamese and Cambodian refugees immigrated to the United States (Martin 1976). As of December 1, 1976, 144,072 Indochinese refugees were resettled in the United States. Of these, 20,400 (16.6 percent) were less than six years of age (U.S. Bureau of the Census 1977). The 1980 Census reported the number of Vietnamese Americans as 261,714. Like Korean Americans, the Vietnamese are widely dispersed, with 46 percent living in the West, 9 percent in the Northeast, 14 percent in the north-central states, and 31 percent in the South. While the discussion here focuses on refugee children, it is important to note that not all Vietnamese residing in the United States have held this status.

Background. The experiences of Vietnamese children in war-torn Southeast Asia and in their new role as refugees in America cannot help but influence their psychological development and learning needs. A former teacher in Vietnam (Dinh 1976) describes several factors, including confrontation with death and evacuation hardships, which have hindered Vietnamese children's adjustment to their new way of life. The wide geographic dispersion of refugees in the United States has accelerated assimilation but interfered with effective administration of educational programs (Burmark and Kim 1978).

Cultural factors and learning characteristics. In addition to language differences, aspects of Vietnamese culture that may influence children's learning include traditional relationships with parents, teachers, and peers; modes of expression, and expectations concerning school. Findings of a seminar with Vietnamese educators indicate that as a group, Vietnamese children are willing students, due possibly to the culture's respect for education and educators (Maldonado 1976). Children's roles in relation to parents are characterized by obedience, and the teacher's status supercedes that of the father (Arizona State Department of Education 1976). Teachers may also find that because children from lower-class families rarely participate in formal education in Vietnam, Vietnamese children may be sensitive to interactions with others of different social level. Moreover, Vietnamese culture emphasizes less direct and open ways of revealing feelings. As a result, children may display considerable uneasiness when required to participate in co-educational activities such as dancing and contact sports (Burmark and Kim 1978).

Amount of previous school experience and expectations about teaching-learning methods may also affect Vietnamese children's behavior in American schools. Due to the sparsity of books and other materials, Vietnamese students are accustomed to learning through rote methods, listening and taking notes, memorization, repetition, and recitation. In the students' former experience, teachers lectured and wrote on the board, rarely asking children to engage in discussion (Dinh 1976; Maldonado 1976). Perhaps the children's passive role in relation to parents and teachers is reflected in the characterization as shy, having respect for elders, and being introspective versus expressive (Arizona State Department of Education 1976). Fewer adjustment problems seem to occur at lower grades where children have had less exposure to traditional forms of Vietnamese education. Parents and children, however, may require preparation for preschool and kindergarten programs. Parents may lack familiarity with the concept of early childhood education since only private schools in Vietnam offered such programs (Maldonado 1976).

As with all other Asian-American groups, broad individual differences exist within the Vietnamese-American population. Children's degree of difference from American expectations may depend on whether they came from urban or rural areas of Vietnam and from intellectual or illiterate families. Attention to time, for example, has been noted to differ between urban and rural children. Finally, it should be remembered that not all Vietnamese children came to America as refugees.

Hawaiians

The 1980 Census counted 167,253 Hawaiians in the United States, 69 percent in Hawaii and 14 percent in California.

Cultural factors. Several authors describe family structure and childrearing practices as important cultural variables in development of Hawaiian children. Data collected in a five-year field study on Hawaiians in Hawaii describe the Hawaiian family as an organized and purposeful socialization system that directs its children toward the ultimate goal of family commitment through useful contribution to the family (Gallimore, Boggs, and Jordan 1974). The outstanding features of the family system are interdependence, shared functioning, and benevolent authoritarianism on the part of the parents. As a consequence, Hawaiian youth learn to approach their elders with respect; make requests in a subtle, indirect manner; and handle authority relationships through group cooperation and avoidance rather than through negotiation with authority figures.

   Learning characteristics. Consistent with cultural role expectations and family emphasis on interdependence, Hawaiian children appear to develop behavioral styles characterized by avoidance of confrontation and motivation for shared versus individual achievement. These culture-based styles bring Hawaiian students into conflict with the school (Gallimore, Boggs, and Jordan 1974). Compared to Anglo-Americans, Hawaiian children have been found to make fewer direct verbal requests of adults outside the home and to work harder and longer for group rather than individual rewards (Gallimore 1972). There is also evidence that need for affiliation rather than need for achievement may be a more significant motivation for Hawaiians (Gallimore 1972). Preliminary research findings suggest that systematic use of positive reinforcement, peer pressure, and reduced use of negative control practices may be useful in modifying the school behavior of Hawaiian children and increasing class productivity (Sloggett 1969).

   In addition to differences in cultural values, language differences displayed by some Hawaiian children may put them at a disadvantage in Anglo-American-oriented schools. In a careful study on standard English (SE) and nonstandard Hawaiian English (NHE) speakers in fifth grade, it was demonstrated that teachers consistently had lower expectations for NHE speakers. However, these children did not develop intellectual deficiencies as a result of an "inferior" language (Choy and Dodd 1976). Academic difficulties manifested by NHE children were at least partially a result of inexperience with the SE-oriented school situation.

Samoans

   The Samoans represent the smallest of the Asian- and Pacific-American subgroups discussed here, with a 1980 Census figure of 42,050. The majority live in California and Hawaii.

Very little written information is available on the childrearing practices and learning characteristics of Samoan people. Munoz (1976) suggests that many Pacific Islanders (Samoan and Guamanian) who migrate to the continental United States are not prepared to cope with the complexities of industrial society. Island society is characterized as one of mutual aid, nontechnical, nonindustrial, and noncompetitive, contrary to values espoused by mainland educational systems. In describing differences among several cultural groups on creativity, one observer describes Western Samoan culture as suppressing creative and independent thinking from birth (Torrance 1962). Samoan teachers seem to highly value quietness and remembering well in pupils. Compared to teachers of other cultures, Samoan teachers find such traits as adventurousness, being a self-starter, curiosity, determination, and self-sufficiency as less important for students. Factors Torrance suggests as underlying these patterns include a strong patriarchal family system and acceptance of authority relationships. It is not clear, however, to what extent these findings can be generalized to Samoan children now living in the United States.

Asian-American Education Project

Only one study devoted specifically to the learning characteristics of preschool age Asian-American children was found: The Asian-American Education Project (Chan, Takanishi, and Kitano 1975). Its purpose was to determine similarities and differences in Asian-American children's learning styles and competencies before they entered public school. The sample consisted of 17 Hawaiian, 18 Chinese-, 22 Japanese-, 18 Korean-, and 16 Filipino-American children, all between the ages of four and five. Procedures for collecting data included structured mother-child observations and child testing.

Structured mother-child observations

These observations were designed to characterize mother-child interactions in a structured teaching situation. Quality and frequency of mothers' verbal and nonverbal assistance, reinforcement, and attention to the child's activity, as well as the child's responses and attention to the mother, were recorded. Data analyzed for Chinese, Japanese, and Korean samples revealed wide within-group differences. As a result, no patterns of mother-child behavior could be derived that would apply to each mother-child pair in an ethnic group. These results again question the practice of dealing with Asian groups as homogenous entities.

Child testing

Test data described children's performance on measures of learning style, perceptual-motor skill, and quantitative concepts.

Two types of learning style, field independence-dependence and conceptual tempo, were assessed. The dimension of field independence-dependence concerns individual variations in amount of differentiation in a perceptual field. Field independence has been positively related to task-oriented behavior and reading success. Field dependence has been correlated with sensitivity to social cues and incidental learning (Keogh 1973). Preliminary analysis of project data suggested that Hawaiian, Chinese-, Japanese-, and Korean-American children's mean field independence scores were similar across groups and compared well to scores for same-age middle class Anglo-American children. The results may be interpreted as indicating that, in general, Asian-American children in these ethnic groups enter school with a well-formulated field-independent perceptual style. Filipino children in the sample tended to be more field dependent than children in other groups.

Conceptual tempo, or the dimension of reflectivity-impulsivity, concerns the degree to which an individual reflects on alternative solutions when several are simultaneously available. An impulsive response style has been related to reading difficulties and problem-solving inefficiency, and its assessment may be useful for early identification of potential learning problems (Epstein, Hallahan, and Kauffman 1975). The data suggest that the Chinese-American children in general demonstrated a slower tempo, or were more reflective, than any other group. Hawaiian children were the next most reflective, followed by Japanese-, Korean-, and Filipino-American children. Boys in the Chinese-American sample tended to be more reflective than girls and took nearly twice the time to respond compared to males in other ethnic groups. Japanese-American and Hawaiian girls, however, tended to have more reflective responses than their male counterparts.

In general, children in the study exhibited normal perceptual-motor development, as indicated on a task requiring reproduction of abstract forms. In one area of visual development (matching identical forms), Filipino students scored slightly lower than children in the other groups and the standardization sample. As a whole, however, the Asian-American children tested well compared to standardization norms, demonstrating competence in form discrimination.

A second visual discrimination task involving letter and number recognition and discrimination revealed wide within-group differences. These may have been due to variations in English language proficiency. The overall sample mean fell within the 49th percentile on norms, although scores for a large proportion of the sample fell above and below that marker. These findings suggest that Asian-American preschoolers vary normally on symbol recognition and discrimination, with some performing well and some poorly. In general, it appears that while Asian-American children were able to discriminate forms, figures, letters, and numbers, matching verbal labels to letters and numbers in English presented some difficulty for them.

The third area of child testing was quantitative concepts. Children were administered a preschool instrument designed to assess mastery of (a) correspondence between numbers of objects and their symbolic numerical representation, (b) comparative and relational terms (e.g., *largest* and *smallest*), and (c) numerical concepts (e.g., *more, most, least, fewest*). A rough comparison between sample children's mean scores and normative data for preschool and kindergarten children suggests that Asian-American children in general have achieved an average or better level of quantitative concept development by the time they reach school age. By group, mean scores for Filipino-, Japanese-, and Chinese-American children exceeded that for kindergarten norms. As a whole, the Korean-American sample scored just under the kindergarten norm, while the Hawaiian children achieved slightly below the preschool average.

Implications for education

The available research on Asian Americans and preliminary data from the Asian-American Education Project reveal three general findings. First, Asian-American cultural groups possess distinct value clusters that influence school behavior and frequently bring children into conflict with the dominant Anglo-American culture of the school. Second, although they are similar in many respects, historical, cultural, and learning differences exist *between* Asian-American groups. Hence, it is inaccurate to consider Asian Americans as a single homogeneous ethnic group. Third, *within* each group there are wide individual differences. With consideration to the tentative nature of contributing data, this section will review the major findings and suggest educational implications for each.

Culture conflict

Value differences between cultural groups may lead to conflict, especially where Asian-American children's behavior fails to conform to the expectations of schools that represent the dominant culture. Cultural values may affect children's motivation, personality, and language. The Hawaiian culture, for example, appears to value group as opposed to individual achievement. As a result, Hawaiian children tend to be more motivated to work for group rather than individual rewards. Hawaiian children's preference for cooperative or shared work challenges the school's demands for individual competition and independence. In the area of personality, available literature suggests that Chinese, Japanese, and Samoan cultural expectations for obedience foster conforming, dependent children. Moreover, it is possible that mother-child interactions that fail to emphasize verbal behavior may predispose Japanese children to restrict verbal participation in classroom situations. With regard to language, Asian-American children, particularly recent immigrants and nonstandard Hawaiian English speakers, face barriers in English-dominant schools.

Two opposing teaching approaches have been suggested in the literature to deal with discrepancies between the child's culture and that of the school. The "cultural deficit" viewpoint advocates changing the *child* to conform to the school's demands. Supporters of this approach contend that school is a preparation for life and as such, must encourage children to adopt styles that will lead to success in a competitive, dominant-culture world. In contrast, the "cultural difference" perspective suggests that *teaching practices* be altered to meet the child's needs. According to the difference viewpoint, cultural patterns, including language and motivational sets that deviate from the Anglo-American norm, are different but equally valid and acceptable. Both approaches to education of culturally different children have advantages and disadvantages. Should the teacher attempt to anglicize Asian-American children in terms of motivation, personality, and language in order to facilitate success in an Anglo-dominant world? Or should the teacher accept the child's existing characteristics and use them to advance learning?

While there certainly is room for compromise, the decision is a serious one and can have profound effects on the child's life in and beyond school. For this reason, parents should be consulted in establishing the child's educational program. A structured, carefully planned interview should be conducted to determine parents' objectives for their child and what they perceive to be the school's role in meeting these objectives.

Some Vietnamese-American parents express concern that their children will lose traditional patterns of behavior such as respect for their fathers and ancestors (Maldonado 1976). Korean-American parents also want their children to continue studying Korean language and culture (Hahn and Dobb 1975). For these and other Asian-American groups, there appears to be a definite need for a bilingual, bicultural program that would facilitate acquisition of English while maintaining and improving native language skill and cultural pride. Inclusion of parents as consultants and as volunteer classroom aides may help provide continuity between school and home in values and behavioral expectations. Meetings with specific groups of Asian-American parents may expose common concerns and help educators give support to the children and the parents themselves. For example, teachers may, upon request, demonstrate methods of reinforcing children's verbal behavior for groups of parents who express concern over their children's verbal participation in school.

Where Asian-American children live in areas isolated from others of the same ethnic group, a bilingual traveling teacher may be an appropriate way to deliver services to several isolated families of the same ethnic group (Hahn and Dobb 1975). Consistent with the need for parent involvement noted above, the traveling teacher interviews the children, conducts educational testing in both English and the native language, and meets with the child's parents. Based on information thus derived, the teacher plans and implements individual instructional programs, spending one day a week at each child's school. Homework assignments given in the native language allow parents to help their children and become more involved in their education. The traveling teacher also provides in-service training for the children's regular teachers to improve their awareness of the children's background and to help them better relate.

Between-group differences

Studies on different Asian-American cultures refute the common tendency to view Asian Americans as a single entity. Asian-American groups may differ from each other in background characteristics, affective traits, learning style, school readiness, and in other areas not yet investigated. In considering the various characteristics that researchers have attributed to individual Asian-American groups, it is important to caution that non-Asian Americans (Anglo-Americans, Blacks) usually have been used as the comparative sample. Hence, while only one Asian-American group is reported as displaying a certain set of characteristics, it is possible that other Asian Americans exhibit a similar set. Nevertheless, until further research demonstrates that the traits studied are shared by many Asian Americans, it will be assumed that these attributes can at present be applied only to the population studied.

Background characteristics. The "model minority" stereotype often leads educators to believe that Asian-American children begin school with many advantages due to the economic and educational success of their parents. As suggested by census and Asian-American Education Project data, however, parental occupation and education differ by cultural group. Moreover, children from different cultural groups may have had different immigration experiences that might also affect school behavior. The special situation of Vietnamese children is a case in point. As noted earlier, Vietnamese children who lived in or near the war-stricken area may demonstrate overly shy and unstable behavior. Those who were confined to refugee camps and had negative contact with American military police may avoid or be wary of Americans. Teachers need to understand these children's background experiences and treat them with patience, encouragement, and friendliness (Dinh 1976).

Affective traits. The review of literature points to the possible existence of affective sets that may characterize certain

Asian-American groups and have implications for instructional practices. Appeals to family honor and awarding of social praise, for example, may be motivating to Filipino-American children who value social responsibility and approval. Similarly, teachers might accommodate to Hawaiian children's group orientation by presenting new concepts or reinforcing learned concepts through group projects. Individual art projects may be varied with cooperative ones, such as a joint mural. Children could work with partners in completing reading and arithmetic exercises. Group and affilitative tendencies can also be used to motivate desirable behavior. Children who reach their achievement objectives might be rewarded with permission to participate in team games. In addition, an individual child's behavior (e.g., seat-sitting) perhaps can be improved if the entire class's receipt of reward (e.g., free time) is contingent upon that child's improvement. In general, demand for competition should be relaxed and group achievement emphasized.

Studies on between-group differences in self-concept may also have implications for classroom behavior. Several tentative suggestions can be drawn from the findings that Korean-American children may possess a relatively low self-concept for popularity and physical appearance. Korean-American children's small numbers encourage constant comparison with Anglo-American rather than other Korean-American children. As a result, Korean-American children may feel that they are physically different and therefore less popular. Instilling a sense of pride in children from minority groups can help elevate self-concept. Activities such as group discussions, self-exploration, and celebrations of cultural events may help children understand and appreciate how people are different (Chang 1975).

Learning styles. While tentative in nature, results of several investigations point to differences among Asian-American groups in approaches to learning. Awareness of these differences may aid teachers in determining appropriate instructional strategies. It will be recalled, for example, that investigations of Western Samoan and bilingual Chinese children suggest that these children may have difficulty with certain aspects of creativity. To the extent that these findings can be generalized to Samoan and Chinese children living in the United States, several activities may be implemented to stimulate creativity. First, demands for structure and rigidity can be reduced and emphasis on correctness and conformity diminished at appropriate times. Group problem solving and brainstorming over common concerns may be introduced to encourage flexibility and fluency in thinking. Children might also be asked to examine interesting pictures or objects to stimulate creative writing. Acceptance of all ideas and reward for productivity versus accuracy can also enhance creative thinking.

As suggested by preliminary data on cognitive styles from the Asian-American Education Project, Filipino-American preschoolers may be more field dependent than other Asian-American children. Second, Chinese-American children may enter school with a highly reflective response style, taking a relatively long time to answer questions. The major implication of these findings is that teachers must recognize that differences may exist between Asian-American groups in learning strategies. A wide repertoire of instructional methods will be needed to provide the best match between a child's cognitive style and the teaching technique. Educators must be sensitive to the idea that different children may require different methods. Field dependent children, for example, might be sensitive to social cues and be more susceptible to incidental learning and contextual elements. Teachers may need to allow extra time for reflective Chinese-American children to respond to questions. Exercises which demand immediate reactions should be avoided except where slow decision making is deemed maladaptive.

Finally, some educational considerations can be derived from recent descriptive literature on learning styles of Vietnamese refugees. The passive role of students in Vietnamese schools may influence the expectations for Vietnamese children in America. For children who have experienced school in Vietnam, a gradual transition is required from rote memorization, copying, and recitation to American expectations for discussion and initiative in learning. A teacher's insistence on immediate adaptation to unfamiliar American methods will create frustration and humiliation (Maldonado 1976). Initial use of rote techniques with gradual addition of other approaches can help Vietnamese-American students adjust. Younger children who have not experienced school in Vietnam will adapt more easily to American schooling. Parent counseling may be beneficial, however, because parents may retain their previous expectations for their children's educational experiences.

School readiness. Asian-American Education Project data indicate that as a whole, Asian-American children enter school with a good grasp of the visual discrimination skills and quantitative concepts important for school readiness. Preliminary analyses by group, however, suggest that Filipino-American children in the sample had more difficulty in visual discrimination than other groups. Hawaiian children performed slightly lower than the norms for quantitative concept development. Although correlational analyses have not yet been done, it is possible that the children's lower performance may have been related to a shorter time of school-type experience. Again, the implication is that teachers should be prepared to expect differences in readiness for school. Asian-American preschoolers having difficulty with skills prerequisite for reading and arithmetic should be given supportive help. They should not be ignored under the expectation that all will be successful achievers without assistance.

A final point about between-group differences merits comment: despite some shared customs, Japanese, Chinese, Filipino, Vietnamese, Korean, Hawaiian, and Samoan people do have different languages and may celebrate different cultural events. Well-intentioned educators commonly assume that recognizing the Chinese Lunar New Year or making *origami* decorations satisfies the objective of cultural awareness for *all* Asian-American students. Yet these activities are not relevant to some Asian-American groups. Exploring a separate aspect of culture for each Asian group represented in the classroom may enhance the individuality of all children and help them recognize their own value as human beings.

Within-group differences

The third major finding of this review was that individual differences exist within each Asian-American group. Investigations of children within a group reveal child-by-child differences that cross-cultural studies tend to mask. For example, comparisons among ethnicities suggest that Japanese Americans as a group tend to be conservative and inhibited. Yet some Japanese Americans are outgoing and assertive. Child test data from the Asian-American Education Project can be interpreted as indicating that each Asian group exhibits a variety of skill levels depending on the individual child's attributes. English versus an Asian language dominance, for instance, may contribute to within-group variation in letter recognition. Observations of mother-child interactions in the same study also demonstrated greater within- than between-group differences in maternal teaching styles. Such intragroup variation requires that teachers consider children's cultural backgrounds and at the same time recognize each child as an individual whose characteristics may or may not fall within the norms for her or his cultural group.

A final word

The study of Asian-American early education has been limited and unsystematic, with few apparent attempts to interrelate and build upon existing knowledge. Moreover, the literature's preliminary nature precludes drawing firm conclusions and advocacy of definitive teaching practices. Yet taken together, the available studies suggest some general methods that offer educators a place to begin in teaching Asian-American children. Discretion must be exercised in generalizing use of these practices until their efficacy is confirmed through research. Until specific instructional techniques have been developed and validated, educators can enhance the school experience of Asian-American children in several ways. Educators must become sensitive to special needs, for example in the areas of language and self-concept. Much can be learned about historical, cultural, and stylistic factors that influence Asian-American children's school behavior. Finally, it is imperative to recognize and treat Asian-American children as the individuals that they truly are.

References

Aldaba-Lim, E., and Javillonar, G. V. "Achievement Motivation in Filipino Entrepreneurship." *International Social Science Journal* 20 (1968): 397–409.

Arizona State Department of Education. *Some Hints to Work with Vietnamese Students.* Urbana, Ill.: ERIC Clearinghouse on ECE, 1976. (ERIC Document Reproduction Service No. ED 133 383)

Ayabe, H. I., and Santo, S. "Conceptual Tempo and the Oriental American." *The Journal of Psychology* 81 (1972): 121–123.

Borke, H., and Sue, S. "Perception of Emotional Responses to Social Interactions by Chinese and American Children." *Journal of Cross-Cultural Psychology* 3 (1972): 309–314.

Burmark, L., and Kim, H. "The Challenge of Educating Vietnamese

Children in American Schools." *Integrated Education* 91 (1978): 2–8.

Caudill, W. "Tiny Dramas: Vocal Communication Between Mother and Infant in Japanese and American Families." In *Mental Health Research in Asia and the Pacific*, Vol. 2, ed. W. Lebra. Honolulu: East-West Center Press, 1971.

Caudill, W., and Frost, L. "A Comparison of Maternal Care and Infant Behavior in Japanese-American, American, and Japanese Families." In *Influences on Human Development*, ed. U. Bronfenbrenner. Hinsdale, Ill.: Dryden Press, 1972.

Caudill, W., and Weinstein, H. "Maternal Care and Infant Behavior in Japan and America." *Psychiatry* 32 (1969): 12–43.

Chan, K. S.; Takanishi, R.; and Kitano, M. K. *An Inquiry into Asian American Preschool Children and Families in Los Angeles*. University of California, Los Angeles, 1975. (ERIC Document Reproduction Service No. ED 117 251)

Chang, T. S. "The Self-Concept of Children in Ethnic Groups: Black American and Korean American." *Elementary School Journal* 76, no. 1 (1975): 52–58.

Chen, J., and Goon, S. W. "Recognition of the Gifted from among Disadvantaged Asian Children." *The Gifted Child Quarterly* 20, no. 2 (1976): 157–164.

Choy, S. J., and Dodd, D. H. "Standard-English-Speaking and Non-standard Hawaiian-English-Speaking Children: Comprehension of Both Dialects and Teacher's Evaluations." *Journal of Educational Psychology* 68, no. 2 (1976): 184–193.

Darsie, M. L. "The Mental Capacity of American-Born Japanese Children." *Comparative Psychology Monographs* 3, no. 15 (1926).

Dinh, V. P. "A Vietnamese Child in Your Classroom?" *Instructor* 85, no. 7 (1976): 86.

Epstein, M. H.; Hallahan, D. P.; and Kauffman, J. M. "Implications of the Reflectivity-Impulsivity Dimension for Special Education." *Journal of Special Education* 9, no. 1 (1975): 11–25.

Gallimore, R. "Variations in the Motivational Antecedents of Achievement among Hawaii's Ethnic Groups." In *Transcultural Research in Mental Health*, Vol. 2, ed. W. Lebra. Honolulu: University of Hawaii Press, 1972.

Gallimore, R.; Boggs, J. W.; and Jordan, C. *Culture, Behavior and Education: A Study of Hawaiian-Americans*. Beverly Hills, Calif.: Sage Publications, 1974.

Graham, V. T. "The Intelligence of Chinese Children in San Francisco." *Journal of Comparative Psychology* 6 (1926): 42–69.

Guthrie, G. M. *The Filipino Child and Philippine Society*. Manila: Philippine University Press, 1961.

Hahn, M., and Dobb, F. "Lost in the System: Korean Students in San Francisco." *Integrated Education* 13, no. 4 (1975): 14–16.

Keogh, B. K. "Perceptual and Cognitive Styles: Implications for Special Education." In *The First Review of Special Education*, Vol. I, ed. L. Mann and D. Sabatino. Philadelphia: JSE Press, 1973.

Kitano, H. H. L. "Japanese-American Mental Illness." In *Asian-Americans: Psychological Perspectives*, ed. S. Sue and N. Wagner. Ben Lomond, Calif.: Science and Behavior Books, 1973.

Kitano, H. H. L. *Race Relations*. Englewood Cliffs, N.J.: Prentice-Hall, 1974.

Kriger, S. F., and Kroes, W. H. "Child-Rearing Attitudes of Chinese, Jewish, and Protestant Mothers." *The Journal of Social Psychology* 86 (1972): 205–210.

Kubany, E. S.; Gallimore, R.; and Buell, J. "The Effects of Extrinsic Factors on Achievement-Oriented Behavior: A Non-Western Case." *Journal of Cross-Cultural Psychology* 1, no. 1 (1970): 77–84.

Livesay, T. M. "Racial Comparisons in Test-Intelligence." *American Journal of Psychology* 55 (1942): 90–95.

Maldonado, S. *Programmatic Recommendations and Considerations in Assisting School Districts to Serve Vietnamese Children*. Urbana, Ill.: ERIC Clearinghouse on Early Childhood Education, 1976. (ERIC Document Reproduction Service No. ED 133 405)

Martin, J. "Vietnamese Students and Their American Advisors." *Change* 8, no. 10 (1976): 30–32.

Moritsugu, J. N. "A Comparative Study of Japanese-American and Caucasian-American Mother-Child Interaction." Senior honors thesis, University of Hawaii, 1971.

Munoz, F. U. "Pacific Islanders in the U.S." *Civil Rights Digest* 9, no. 1 (1976): 42–43.

Pitler, B. "Chicago's Korean American Community." *Integrated Education* 88 (1977): 44–47.

"Preliminary 1980 Census Results." *Pacific/Asian American Mental Health Research Center Research Review* 1, no. 1 (1982): 9.

Sloggett, B. B. "Behavior Modification of the Underachieving Rural Hawaiian: An Experimental Classroom." *Pacific Anthropological Records* No. 5. Honolulu: Department of Anthropology, B. P. Bishop Museum, 1969.

Sloggett, B. B.; Gallimore, R.; and Kubany, E. S. "A Comparative Analysis of Fantasy Need Achievement among High and Low Achieving Male Hawaiian-Americans." *Journal of Cross-Cultural Psychology* 1, no. 1 (1970): 53–61.

Steward, M., and Steward, D. "The Observation of Anglo-, Mexican-, and Chinese-American Mothers Teaching Their Young Sons." *Child Development* 44 (1973): 329–337.

Stodolsky, S. S., and Lesser, G. "Learning Patterns in the Disadvantaged." *Harvard Educational Review* 37 (1967): 546–593.

Sue, D. W. "Ethnic Identity: The Impact of Two Cultures on the Psychological Development of Asians in America." In *Asian-Americans: Psychological Perspectives*, ed. S. Sue and N. Wagner. Ben Lomond, Calif.: Science and Behavior Books, 1973.

Sue, D. W., and Kirk, B. A. "Psychological Characteristics of Chinese-American Students." *Journal of Counseling Psychology* 19 (1972): 471–478.
Sue, S.; Sue, D. W.; and Sue, D. W. "Asian Americans as a Minority Group." *American Psychologist* 30, no. 9 (1975): 906–910.
Symonds, P. "The Effect of Attendance at Chinese Language Schools on Ability with English Language." *Journal of Applied Psychology* 8 (1924a): 411–423.
Symonds, P. "The Intelligence of Chinese in Hawaii." *School and Society* 19 (1924b): 442.
Torrance, E. P. "Cultural Discontinuities and the Development of Originality of Thinking." *Exceptional Children* 29 (1962): 2–13.
Torrance, E. P.; Wu, J.; Gowan, J. C.; and Aliotti, N. C. "Creative Functioning of Monolingual and Bilingual Children in Singapore." *Journal of Educational Psychology* 60, no. 1 (1970): 72–75.
U.S. Bureau of the Census. *Statistical Abstracts of the United States: 1977* (98th edition). Washington, D.C.: U.S. Bureau of the Census, 1977.
Yee, L. Y., and LaForge, R. "Relationship Between Mental Abilities, Social Class, and Exposure to English in Chinese Fourth Graders." *Journal of Educational Psychology* 66, no. 6 (1974): 826–834.
Yeung, K. T. "The Intelligence of Chinese Children in San Francisco and Vicinity." *Journal of Applied Psychology* 5 (1921): 267–274.
Young, N. F. "Changes in Values and Strategies among Chinese in Hawaii." *Sociology and Social Research* 56, no. 2 (1972): 228–241.
Yu, C. Y. "The 'Others.'" *Civil Rights Digest* 9, no. 1 (1976): 44–51.

Revised from an earlier version that appeared in *Young Children* 36, no. 2 (January 1980): 13–26. ©1980 by the National Association for the Education of Young Children, 1834 Connecticut Ave., N.W., Washington, DC 20009.

Rosario C. Gingras

5
Early Childhood Bilingualism:
Some Considerations from Second-Language Acquisition Research

In the absence of sociopathic circumstances, normal children will almost inevitably master at least one natural language. Given an appropriate set of circumstances, normal children can also master a second or third language. How children achieve mastery in a second language is the subject of much research. Although considerable work remains, findings to date indicate directions that early childhood educators should consider carefully.

Language competence and performance

One of the most important distinctions in modern linguistics, derived from the transformational-generative grammar theory, is the distinction between *competence* and *performance*. Competence refers to the implicit knowledge a speaker has of the rules of the language. Performance refers to speech, but all speakers make errors in their speech. When such errors occur, the speaker will often correct them. The ability to correct errors is seen by the linguist as evidence that competence is distinct from performance. It is this implicit knowledge of a language that is the object of linguistic research. A bilingual speaker will have achieved competence and performance in two languages.

Research on linguistic competence is necessarily indirect because the language competence is not directly observable but must be inferred from performance. While the distinction between competence and performance might seem esoteric, this difference accounts for the difficulty linguists have in attempting to give answers to seemingly simple questions such as, "How many words does a child of five know?"

The vocabulary of any speaker of a given language can only be inferred from observing the speaker use language in meaningful contexts. The vocabulary purported to be known by a given subject will be limited to that actually observed in the speech of the subject or elicited directly by the observer. No speaker, regardless of age, uses all of her or his vocabulary with equal frequency. Thus, word counts are based on a limited sample of the total vocabulary known by a given speaker. Since linguists cannot determine what a speaker might know beyond what can be determined from performance, it follows that research findings and results from language competency assessment instruments may be inaccurate and possibly misleading. This does not mean that we ought to ignore such findings but rather that we should take care in interpreting such results because vocabulary surveys may be useful aids in language studies.

Language development

The language that is first mastered in childhood is often referred to as the *mother tongue, native language,* or *first language.* The pace at which children acquire their first language appears to vary considerably. It is not clear in what ways differences in acquisition rates correlate with other developmental characteristics. While it has been assumed that early first-language acquisition indicates high intelligence, this may not be so. For example, Einstein is reputed to have begun speaking at age four. Part of the problem in correlating developmental stages in first-language acquisition with other physiological developments is related to the nature of the complexity of language as well as to the significant gaps that exist in the available descriptive studies of language development.

Extensive studies document the developmental stages of first-language acquisition from birth to five years. Much of this literature is reviewed in Snow and Ferguson (1977). The number of studies of first-language acquisition between the ages of five and adulthood is quite limited. Most linguistic studies focus on adult speech and there is considerable agreement on the type of phonological, syntactic, and semantic structures adult speakers are known to have. There is also a considerable degree of agreement on the types and sequencing of linguistic structures learned by young children. However, little research exists on the development of a first language for children between five and adolescence.

The speech of a four-year-old and that of an adult speaking the same language contain both qualitative and quantitative differences. These include differences in vocabulary (lexicon), syntax, and semantics. Semantic structures such as generic sentences, for example, "Beavers build dams," do not appear in young children's speech. It is not clear at what age children begin to master such structures.

During the 1950s structuralist linguists popularized the notion that a child masters most of the grammatical and sound systems of the first language by age five. Indeed, the average child masters a considerable amount of language by age five (Hockett 1958):

■ the main phonological contrasts, or surface phonemic differences, in the language sound system
■ the bulk of the inflectional system
■ the rules for the major syntactic structures
■ a considerable vocabulary

Compared to the speech of an adult, a five-year-old's speech has much to be developed. Complex systems such as derivations (the system that relates lexical items, for example, *telegraphy, telegraphic*), presuppositions (such as are inherent in a sentence of the type, "Have you stopped beating your wife?"), and foregrounding (which accounts for the differences between "Smoking causes cancer" and "What causes cancer is smoking") are typical of adult speech. Just when children learn such structures remains an open question.

First-language research appears to focus on the acquisition of English. As of 1976, there were approximately 20 longitudinal case studies of children acquiring English as a first language, some of which will be discussed here. There were reported longitudinal studies of children acquiring Spanish as a first language (Montes-Giraldo 1967; Peronard 1977). Longitudinal studies of the acquistion of two languages have been reported also (Ferguson 1973). Cross-sectional studies of first-language acquisition for many languages exist, but longitudinal studies supply the best evidence for the types and sequencing of structures acquired, because children vary considerably in the rate of language acquisition.

Research on the acquisition of English as a first language indicates that children appear to follow the same sequencing patterns as followed in other languages. For example, mastery of sound contrasts tends to follow universal sequences: if a language has an *r* sound, such a sound will be distinguished from other sounds very late; it will probably be the final sound contrast mastered. In fact, for a language such as Spanish, the inability to produce an *r* sound clearly is taken as evidence of childish speech.

Of particular interest to early childhood educators is the research that has been conducted in relation to the critical period for language acquisition. While all normal children can be expected to acquire a first language, under unfortunate circumstances some children fail to do so. If children are not exposed to any speech, they fail to acquire language. Such unfortunate children have been studied (see Curtiss 1977) and it has been concluded that if children are deprived of normal linguistic exposure during the critical period from very early childhood to around puberty, these children will probably not learn a language (Lenneberg 1967). While the number of children who have been reported not to have mastered a first language because of sociopathological circumstances is small, other evidence of an indirect sort appears to support the critical period hypothesis.

Many of these facets of language study—vocabulary, rate of language acquisition, sequencing of phonemic and morphological language skills, and the innate ability to acquire language—are useful and equally valid in studies of second-language acquisition.

Defining bilingualism

Although the term *bilingual* is commonly used, it lacks a generally agreed-upon definition. Haugen (1972) defined bilingualism as "knowledge of two languages," but did not specify how much of either language has to be known in order to be bilingual. Given the complexity of any language, it is unlikely that a general definition for *fluent speaker* can be given.

This lack of general consensus as to what constitutes bilingualism is particularly problematic in the case of child-bilingualism. Such children may have differing levels of competence (relative to other children their age) in their two languages perhaps because of differences in the settings in which the two languages were learned. Thus, early childhood bilinguals may be able to do different things with each language. Also, early childhood bilinguals may not have developed either of their languages to the degree that monolingual children of the same age do. A bilingual dominance test will probably not uncover such differences. A bilingual child may well be weak in both languages but stronger in one than the other. It is unfortunate that there is so much stress on dominance tests in bilingual education programs. The use of such instruments with young children is not recommended.

How children acquire a second language

According to Hockett (1958), young children appear to learn a second language in much the same way they learn their first. Ravem (1978) finds that the acquisition of the second language occurs independently of the first language. Padilla and Leibman (1975) conclude that parallel development occurs in both languages and that children appear able and willing to keep two languages apart. Huang and Hatch (1979) report that children acquiring a second language go through a silent period during which time they appear to be very quiet in the classroom while building up competence in the second language. During such times, children may not be willing to produce speech in the second language, but by use of gestures as well as responses in the first language they will give evidence that they do understand. Such children will communicate in the second language when they feel the time is right. To insist that children start speaking in the second language during these silent periods may be counterproductive.

The observation that second-language acquistion is similar to first-language acquisition among young children may be supported by the phenomenon Krashen (1978) called *caretaker language* (language behavior that adults conform to when dealing with young children). The outstanding features of caretaker language as noted by Krashen are listed below.

1. Its purpose is not explicitly to *teach* language to young

children but to help them understand the meaning of what is being communicated.

2. It deals with the here and now.

3. It uses short simple sentences that become more complex as children grow older.

4. It uses slightly more complex sentences than children are using.

5. Caretaker speakers repeat syntactic patterns frequently.

6. Caretaker speakers slow down by pausing longer.

Caretaker language presents language in a form that can serve as input for the child's language acquisition. This suggests that teaching young children a second language in the same manner in which they were taught their first—with caretaker language—is most effective. Further studies of caretaker language, with emphasis on vocabularies used by adult caretakers, and the particular syntactic structuring which is most effective in helping children acquire a second language might reveal much about the universal features of language acquisition.

When children acquire a second language

Just as the pace of first-language acquisition will vary considerably, the rate at which children may learn a second language will also vary. Although the processes of learning languages may be identical, the intricacies of relating a newly acquired language to a first language are complex.

In general, the younger a child is when exposed to a second language in an appropriate setting, the more likely it is that the child will acquire competence in the second language with nativelike fluency. However, once puberty is reached, an individual exposed to a second language will probably not master it completely. The further past puberty an individual learns a second language, the more likely it is that the individual will speak the second language with a noticeable accent (for a full discussion, see Krashen 1973). Consequently, there appears to be consensus that a second language should be learned before puberty if nativelike fluency is desired.

How much sooner than puberty second-language instruction should begin remains an open question. Cummins (1979) suggests that there is a "developmental interdependence" between the development of competence in a second language and the first-language competence at the time when intensive exposure to the second language begins. Current research indicates that children can begin to acquire a second language at a very early age. However, it is not clear if early bilingualism is necessarily good for the child's linguistic development. As Sagan (1977) has observed, "absence of evidence is not the same as evidence of absence."

Clearly, additional research is needed to determine how early a child should be exposed to a second language in order to derive the greatest benefit from bilingualism. At present it is generally believed that children can acquire a second language if exposed to one under appropriate contexts at any time *before* puberty and that if such children are exposed to a second language under favorable circumstances prior to age five, it is almost inevitable that they will acquire the second language with nativelike mastery. This is clearly in conflict with the research results reported by Cummins (1979) and those in Sweden (see Skutnabb-Kangas and Toukomaa 1976). An apparent solution to this conflict is to take a very conservative stand and suggest that the best time to expose children to a second language is when they have mastered the silent features of the first language—around the age of six or so. This suggestion presents a serious problem to the bilingual early childhood educator. While current research does not seem to indicate that very early childhood bilingualism confers positive effects on the bilingual child, neither does this research indicate that early childhood bilingualism necessarily has negative effects.

Summary

Current research is not conclusive concerning the desirability of bilingualism at a very young age. Research findings indicate that children should begin learning a second language before puberty but do not offer insights about how young the child should be. Further, while young children can acquire a second language quite readily, it remains to be seen how desirable early bilingualism is. Much research remains to be done. Researchers such as Padilla, Leibman, and Eugene Garcia are currently working in this area. Perhaps in the research process we will come to understand better how adults might acquire a second language and, ultimately, bilingualism in children and adults will be seen as both a natural and a positive process.

References

Curtiss, S. *Genie: A Psycholinguistic Study of a Modern-Day "Wild Child."* New York: Academic Press, 1977.

Cummins, J. "Linguistic Interdependence and the Educational Development of Bilingual Children." *Review of Educational Research* 49, no. 2 (1979): 222–251.

Ferguson, C. *Studies in Child Language and Development.* New York: Holt, Rinehart & Winston, 1973.

Haugen, E. *The Ecology of Language.* Stanford, Calif.: Stanford University Press, 1972.

Hockett, C. *A Course in Modern Linguistics.* New York: Macmillan, 1958.

Huang, J., and Hatch, E. "A Chinese Child's Acquisition of English." In *Second Language Acquisition,* ed. E. Hatch. Rowley, Mass.: Newbury House, 1979.

Krashen, S. "Formal and Informal Linguistic Environments in Language Learning and Language Acquisition." *TESOL Quarterly* 10 (1973): 157–168.

Krashen, S. "The Monitor Theory." In *Second Language Acquisition and Foreign Language Teaching,* ed. R. C. Gingras. Arlington, Va.: Center for Applied Linguistics, 1978.

Lenneberg, E. *Biological Foundations of Language.* New York: Wiley, 1967.

Montes-Giraldo, J. J. "El Sistema, la Norma y el Aprendizaje de la Lengua." *Boletín del Instituto Caro y Cuervo* (Thesaurus) 31 (1967).

Padilla, A. M., and Leibman, E. "Language Acquisition in the Bilingual Child." *La Revista Bilingüe* [The bilingual review.] 2 (1975): 34–35.

Peronard, M. "Adquisicíon del Lenguaje en un Nino Atipico: Retardo o Desviacíon." *Boletin de Filologia* 28 (1977): 139–152.

Ravem, R. "Two Norweigan Children's Acquisition of English Syntax." In *Second Language Acquisition: A Book of Readings,* ed. E. Hatch. Rowley, Mass.: Newbury House, 1978.

Sagan, C. *The Dragons of Eden.* New York: Random House, 1977.

Snow, C., and Ferguson, C. *Talking to Children.* Cambridge: Cambridge University Press, 1977.

Skutnabb-Kangas, T., and Toukomaa, P. *Teaching Migrant Children's Mother Tongue and Learning the Language of the Host Country in the Context of the Socio-Cultural Situation of the Migrant Family.* Helsinki: The Finnish National Commission for UNESCO, 1976.

II
Educational Practices and Materials

Jeanne B. Morris

Classroom Methods and Materials

Multicultural education, reflecting the diversity of American society, can become a part of the classroom in all programs for young children. Four elements are essential to the development of an effective multicultural education program:

- teacher sensitivity to and knowledge of cultural diversity
- meaningful curriculum activities and experiences
- carefully selected instructional materials
- appropriate instructional resources

The teacher's cultural sensitivity and knowledge

Teachers have a major influence on the development and education of young children. Spodek (1978) states that "directly or indirectly [the teacher] controls much of the activity in the classroom and is responsible for all that occurs for the children during the day" (p. 1). Almy (1975) refers to "the function of teachers of young children as models of behavior" (p. 21). Mussen, Conger, and Kagan (1974) view teachers as significant adults beyond the family who play major roles in the child's development. Dunfee (1969) reports that in an analysis of curriculum implementation the teacher was identified as occupying the crucial role in the success or failure of desired change.

Teachers must have positive attitudes about cultural diversity in order to successfully implement multicultural education in their classrooms. Young children are remarkably sensitive and adult sincerity or insincerity rarely escapes them. Studies of teacher expectations demonstrate that motivating or limiting messages can be indirectly communicated by teach-

77

ers, triggering children's positive or negative self-perceptions and attitudes. Teacher attitudes and behaviors toward anyone who differs to any degree from those in the majority culture become important indicators of the worth of cultural differences. For example, if teachers reject language that varies from the standard, children will learn that nonstandard English is not only unacceptable but bad and deficient. Teachers must accept each child's language style as a part of that child and must work *through* the child's language in the process of education.

In order to provide meaningful experiences and activities in intergroup education for young children, teachers must be familiar with concepts of culture and cultural identification. Information and material about and by Afro-Americans, Mexican-Americans, and members of other cultural groups are often sought to increase and strengthen knowledge backgrounds. Teachers who are themselves members of cultural minority groups often must depend on written information because of the paucity of sources in the past. Teachers should select material carefully to ensure quality and that varying viewpoints are included. Chapter 7 of this book and these resources may be helpful:

Banks, J. A. *Teaching Strategies for Ethnic Studies*, 2nd ed. Boston: Allyn & Bacon, 1979.

Gold, M. J.; Carl, C. A.; and Rivlin, H. N., eds. *In Praise of Diversity: A Resource Book for Multicultural Education*. Washington, D.C.: Teacher Corps/Association of Teacher Educators, 1977.

Grant, C. A., ed. *Multicultural Education: Commitments, Issues, Applications*. Washington, D.C.: Association for Supervision and Curriculum Development, 1977.

Each of these books contains information about culture as well as extensive listings of selected references to enhance teacher awareness.

While teachers can get information from written materials, personal interactions with members of culturally diverse groups are also helpful in developing your awareness of differences in experiences and viewpoints. In addition, informal and formal discussions with colleagues, parents, friends, and resource people who are sensitive to and have knowledge of cultural groups can be instrumental in clarifying understandings and misinterpretations.

Learning experiences for children

Implementing multicultural education requires planning and organizing activities so that new information and concepts of culture can be presented to children as catalysts for positive attitude formation.

Banks (1979) presents four models of curriculum development in multicultural education. The *Anglo-American Model* is one where experiences are presented from the sole perspective of Anglo-Americans. The *Ethnic Additive Model* adds ethnic content, including Black Studies and units on other ethnic groups, to the first model. Experiences provided with the *Multiethnic Model* focus on the study of historical and social events from many ethnic perspectives. Finally, curriculum experiences in the *Ethnonational Model* reflect a multinational perspective.

The *Anglo-American Model*, which still exists in some classrooms, is educationally inappropriate in a culturally diverse society. This model may include stereotyped activities that only help to reinforce negative perceptions of cultural differences. Teachers who wish to change their curriculum or who have limited commitment to teaching about cultural diversity usually move first to the *Ethnic Additive Model*. This model may include curriculum units on intergroup education that focus on Native-American life through activities for making headdresses, tomahawks, and teepees at Thanksgiving time, for example, or on Mexican culture through making piñatas and serapes. Children can also cook and taste foods of other cultural groups. Once cultural groups are introduced they may be ignored for the remainder of the year if teachers feel that they have demonstrated sufficient and appropriate attention to cultural diversity.

Additive approaches that emphasize a single culture are acceptable only (1) when the focus on that culture is not limited to those groups in which there are children in the classroom and (2) when plans are made to use the *Multiethnic Model* within a short time. The study of single cultures often helps teachers to become more knowledgeable about history, customs, and contributions of cultural groups and members of those groups. They are then more able to plan meaningful experiences for children.

Activities that help children to understand the humanness of each individual are especially important in multicultural

education. People throughout the world share the same biological and social needs. Values, customs, and beliefs—culture—determine how those needs are met. The need for food
and shelter is universal. For some people certain foods are more
acceptable than others; housing needs may be met in a variety
of ways. The perceptions of all children are widened when they
are helped to realize that humans are more alike than different
and that cultural differences accommodate the same needs.

When presented in a positive climate, explorations of the
ways people differ can promote acceptance of diversity. For
example, children can make collages and self-portraits, discuss
shared and contrasting interests, and explore variety in the
world. When culturally defined practices for satisfying human
needs are presented positively, the child from a cultural minority group can develop and maintain cultural identity with
pride and the majority child can place her or his culture in
context with others. In this way all children develop an understanding of and respect for diversity.

In studying any single culture, teachers must be careful that
elements of cultural identification are not generalized to *all*
members of the group studied. Members of cultural groups are
individuals who vary in degree of attachment to and/or identification with their groups, although there are common bonds
that unify each group.

Banks (1979) suggests:

> One's attachment and identification with (the group) varies with
> the individual, the times in one's life and the situations and set-
> tings in which one finds himself or herself. Depending on expe-
> riences, social class, and many other variables, ethnicity may be
> very important . . . or unimportant to the individual. Students
> should be helped to understand that just because . . . an individual
> is a member of a particular ethnic group does not mean that that
> individual has a strong identity . . . or that ethnicity is very im-
> portant. . . . (p. 60)

Banks adds:

> We often assume that ethnic groups are monolithic and have
> rather homogeneous needs and characteristics. Rarely is sufficient
> attention given to the enormous differences within ethnic groups.
> We also see ethnic groups as static and unchanging. However,
> ethnic groups within modernized democratic societies are highly
> diverse, complex, and changing entities. (p. 61)

To prevent children from overgeneralizing about any culture

teachers may find it useful to use modifiers such as *some, many, in some parts of the country,* or *in some communities* to help children understand that while the characteristic or concept under study applies generally, it may not apply to each situation, person, or group.

The most positive approach to multicultural education is one where emphasis on single cultures is replaced by the multiethnic orientation using several instructional strategies selected for their appropriateness depending on the developmental level of the children in the group. Classroom environments can be arranged to reflect the valuing of diversity. In an elementary classroom, special interest areas developed from culturally related topics could include one labeled "Cultures All Around Us" displaying artifacts and art pieces. A large map of the United States, for example, could show Indian names for local regions or rivers. Posters of food from other countries which are important parts of our diet can also help the class to focus on diversity. Such creative displays can be developed using student input and involvement even when leadership comes from the teacher. Classroom libraries should include biographies and autobiographies of people from different cultures as well as other multiethnic materials. Initiation strategies such as these do not explain significant aspects of the history, culture, traditions, or experiences of the range of culturally diverse groups. Their primary usefulness is to generate interest and build bridges to the next phase.

The integration of multicultural content into all subject areas presents the second level in building a multicultural curriculum. Walsh (1980) suggests one method for doing this: "After listing the subjects or activities which normally comprise the daily program, the teacher describes at least two activities for each through which a multicultural dimension could be integrated," (p. 247).

During language arts activities, for example, monolingual speakers can be exposed to other language systems and can develop an appreciation for the language of non-English speakers as children engage in open discussions of differences in language. Young children can discover that in some communities and families containers for bringing groceries home are called *sacks* while in others these are called *bags.* Some people turn on a *spigot* to get water while others use a *faucet. Mother, mommie, mom, grandpa,* and *grandfather* are similar but different terms used to identify family members. For some, the evening meal is *dinner* and not *supper*. The musical presentation, "Greetings in Many Languages," (Jenkins, n.d.) delightfully presents diversity in language.

Other activities for children at all levels include explorations of words in the English language that originate from other languages. For example, *ketchup* comes from Malay, *sauerkraut* from German, *mosquito* from Spanish, and *piano* from Italian. Native Americans have contributed *raccoon*, and *cole slaw* comes from the Dutch. Investigating different number and alphabet systems is also a suitable activity and older children can compare writing systems such as Japanese, Chinese, and Hebrew. *Multicultural Teaching* (Tiedt and Tiedt 1979) presents these and numerous other activities which focus on diversity in language.

Multicultural concepts presented in school can encompass race, ethnicity, discrimination, and acculturation/assimilation. Cultural identity must not overshadow the humanness of individuals but it should be recognized. With older elementary children, for example, you can emphasize the contribution of Dr. Charles Drew, a Black American who discovered blood plasma, as a way of making life better for all of humanity and as an accomplishment of a cultural group member who overcame acts of prejudice and discrimination. You can provide literary subjects and materials, music, art, and drama from various cultures to help children know and understand what these forms of expression reveal about a culture.

Experiences that help children to know and appreciate the customs and the history of cultural groups can lead to deep and meaningful levels of understanding. By considering facts and events from a variety of cultural viewpoints, you can expand multicultural education from introductory activities to other areas of curriculum. Teachers can infuse established curriculum content with cultural concepts.

The celebration of holidays, standard in early childhood classes, is an excellent vehicle for including multicutural concepts in the curriculum. The early weeks of November, for example, are spent preparing for Thanksgiving. Yet few children or teachers have considered Thanksgiving from the Native-American point of view. While the Pilgrims' joy of surviving a year in a strange land must be acknowledged, it is equally important to recognize the changes that occurred in the lives of those living in America at the time of the immigration of the Pilgrims and other Europeans. Both perspectives should be explored (see Hirschfelder and Califf 1979 and Ramsey 1979).

Children can learn to recognize significant days that are specific to particular cultural groups; Jewish and Chinese New Years, Puerto Rican Awareness Day, Martin Luther King Day, and Hawaii's Kuhio Day can be celebrated in the classroom as well as Halloween and Easter. Canada's Thanksgiving celebration in October could be compared and contrasted with the U.S. celebration in November. Traditional heroes and celebrations should not be the only references to cultural diversity found in schools. Chronologies of cultural significance can be helpful resources for planning activities related to commemorations and celebrations.

Multicultural curriculum concepts that provide young children with new information about cultural groups can be effective in developing positive attitudes and modifying old ones. Teachers should use strategies related to the needs, interests, abilities, and experiences of the learners. Children in urban, suburban, and rural settings, monocultural or multicultural, all have experiences and backgrounds that differ.

Instructional materials

Instructional materials for multicultural education can focus on single cultures or be multicultural. There are more materials available today that support understanding and acceptance of diversity than were available a decade ago, but they vary greatly in quality. Most are a vast improvement over initial attempts to provide culturally related educational materials. For instance, many books available earlier included illustrations in which colors were added to Anglo characters' features to represent non-Anglo-Americans. More realistic and acceptable illustrations can be found today. Content and plot also reflect more accurately the variety of life styles and cultural patterns in society. Despite these changes, the problem of adequate and suitable instructional material is not completely solved. Materials for children, like those for adults, should not be selected solely because they have culturally related titles, captions, or illustrations, or are authored by members of cultural groups. All instructional materials must adequately serve a variety of sound educational purposes as well.

Guidelines for judging the appropriateness of instructional materials for multicultural education are important. Teachers should evaluate instructional aids for educational value, grade-level appropriateness, interest to students involved, facility of use, and technical quality. Instructional materials for multi-cultural programs must also be judged to determine if they include obvious representation of the many cultures in the society, provide accurate and reliable information about cul-ture and cultural groups, and present diversity as a positive fact of life. In addition, materials should help students to know and appreciate current life styles as well as historical contributions of cultural groups.

Guidelines to judge the suitability of materials for multi-cultural education have been developed by a number of re-sponsible individuals and organizations. Among guidelines that teachers will find helpful are those by Banks (1974) and Dunfee (1976). Other guidelines are available from the Council on Interracial Books for Children, The Anti-Defamation Lea-gue of B'nai B'rith, the American Association of Colleges for Teacher Education, and the Social Science Education Consor-tium (addresses are listed at the end of this chapter). Most state departments of education provide evaluation criteria for judg-ing bias-free instructional materials. *Fair Textbooks: A Re-source Guide* (1979) evaluates often used textbooks and other instructional materials. That volume also includes a statement from the Association of American Publishers expressing con-cern for and response to meeting the challenges of fair and equal representation of all cultures in learning materials.

Once guidelines for evaluating and selecting materials have been established, appropriate materials can be selected. No one kind of instructional material is best and teachers may find combinations of materials effective. Carefully identified teach-ing strategies and diagnoses of learner needs seem to provide the best clues to the selection of materials. Pictures, posters, cultural artifacts, music, literature, and cultural study kits can provide resources for children. Materials developed by children and teachers are equally important in supporting the under-standing of cultural diversity.

Annotated and recommended lists of instructional materials for multicultural programs are available from a number of sources including the Council on Interracial Books for Chil-dren, various library associations (particularly those in New York City and California), the National Association for the

Advancement of Colored People, and Integrated Education Association. Books mentioned earlier (Banks 1974; Tiedt and Tiedt 1979) and ERIC publications provide excellent listings of selected materials for multicultural education. These references include teacher and student awareness materials, profiles of cultural groups and their members, anthologies, biographies, autobiographies, and cross-subject instructional materials. Most suggest age or grade designations. Many have descriptions for making materials or adapting standard classroom materials. Some of these references include lists of free and inexpensive items that cover a wide range of subjects. Publications such as *Young Children, Instructor,* or *Early Years* often feature articles and activities that relate to multicultural education. Teachers must not overlook the usefulness of culturally related publications that send messages to children by their appearance in the classroom and are helpful in developing special projects. Cultural publications are listed in *The Encyclopedic Directory of Ethnic Newspapers and Periodicals in the United States* (Wynar and Wynar 1972). The *Administrators' Checklist for Enhancing Multi-Cultural Curriculum (Multi-Ethnic, Non-Sexist)* (Boyer, n.d.) can be helpful to those who are in positions to influence curriculum development. Administrators especially will find *Curriculum Guidelines for Multiethnic Education* (1976) a valuable tool for assessing total learning environments.

Human resources

A range of human resources can be used in multicultural education including other professionals in the schools, parents, and community resource people. Effective use of resource people requires collaborative efforts. Collaboration develops from sensitivity and knowledge, planning and organizing, sharing, caring, and commitment.

Administrators and program directors can be important agents of change. They can not only promote, but directly and actively campaign for staff development programs to provide opportunities in which multicultural concepts and understandings are questioned, investigated, and clarified. Staff development should involve all staff members who interact with and provide services to children. Administrators must also engage in efforts to attract employees with culturally diverse backgrounds. The leadership of programs for young children must introduce, guide, and support every facet of the process.

Some elementary schools include a range of people: curriculum specialists, assistants, supervisors, librarians, media center staff, and those in noninstructional positions. All these can combine to form strong support systems for classroom teachers, identifying resources and activities and helping teachers to interpret the program to others. This support from the total environment can make multicultural education multidimensional. The nutritionist or dietitian, for example, can plan menus including foods from various cultures. Librarians or media center personnel can coordinate displays and develop kits to coincide with topics under study in the classroom. Resource personnel can secure materials for adults as well as children, and can provide classroom services by sharing their experiences and insights with the children.

Good programs for young children do not operate in isolation from the community; the community can influence, react to, and support a program, contributing to a reciprocal relationship. The community offers many possibilities through which vicarious experiences can be translated into real-life ones.

Information about educational programs often has to be communicated to the public. Captivating brochures or flyers, feature articles in newspapers, and displays at strategic locations, such as store windows or shopping malls, can carry messages into the community focusing on the educational soundness of curriculum concepts. Parents can contribute to these promotional activities. Many approaches and activities effective in introducing parents to multicultural education are also appropriate for informing the community and cultivating its support.

People from the community can be exciting resources in classrooms. Those who are willing to share their expertise and knowledge with children should be involved in the program at appropriate times. People from the community can be effective role models for children, explaining careers and jobs. Interest in the backgrounds of citizens who are members of cultural groups should not be the only reason for their presence in the classroom, however. Their contributions and roles as members of the community at large must also be acknowledged. It is within this context that music, stories, dress, or traditional cultural foods, crafts, and art can be fully shared and appreciated.

Early childhood teachers should continuously survey their communities for opportunities to supplement children's learning experiences. Most communities offer a variety of possibilities for field trips that will strengthen the multicultural curriculum. For example, teachers can take the class to the local library to view displays. Librarians can be helpful in locating books and other materials and identifying areas of the community or places nearby which have some historical or cultural significance. Community centers and museums may have culturally related objects that add dimension to the curriculum. Older classes can visit businesses that employ people of diverse cultural backgrounds. Teachers must be aware of excursions into the community which may work to reinforce prejudices and stereotypes of cultural groups. For example, visiting or passing a section of the community where only one cultural group resides or seeing only members of cultural minority groups in certain occupations can be confusing to young children without explanations. Teachers must be willing and able to explain about prejudice and discrimination in ways young children can understand.

Although the teacher plays the major role in implementing the curriculum, teachers, administrators, and members of the community learn from each other and from the children. Multidimensional and multicultural resources can enrich early childhood experiences and can begin to form a coherent framework for successful multicultural education.

Summary

The primary objective of multicultural education is to affirm cultural diversity by correcting stereotypes, myths, omissions, and distortions by providing accurate accounts of cultural groups as viable entities in American society. A curriculum that attempts to build support of diversity can grow from accepting the similarities and differences among people in positive ways. The success of multicultural methods and materials depends on all who interact with young children. Those who advocate curriculum revision for multicultural education propose that such a revision occur in all schools so that cultural diversity, which characterizes North America, becomes an integral part of the education of every child.

Teachers, administrators, parents, and members of the com-

munity that the school serves must make commitments to
support multicultural education. Williams and Morland (1976)
said it well:

> programming which gives children a realistic view of the Amer-
> ican society can be instrumental in developing an understanding
> of and appreciation for cultural pluralism and in developing ideal
> human relationships (p. 165)

Achieving the goals of multicultural education requires planning that emphasizes a mutual exchange of cultural heritages,
traditions, customs, and current life styles. Teachers must not
apologize for planning to help the children they teach form and
extend greater understanding of and respect for diversity. Each
of us has the right to be respected as an individual and to respect
the individuality of others. Programs for young children have
a responsibility to respond in ways that are consistent with
democratic principles.

Organizations and publishers

Allyn & Bacon
7 Wells Ave.
Newton, MA 02159
617-964-5530

American Association of
  Colleges for Teacher
  Education
1 Dupont Circle, N.W.
Suite 610
Washington, DC 20036
202-293-2450

The Anti-Defamation League
  of B'nai B'rith
823 United Nations Plaza
New York, NY 10017
212-490-2525

Association for Supervision
  and Curriculum
  Development
225 North Washington St.
Alexandria, VA 22314
703-549-9110

Association of Teacher
  Educators
1900 Association Dr.
Reston, VA 22091
703-620-3110

California Library Association
717 K St.
Suite 300
Sacramento, CA 95814
916-447-8541

Council on Interracial Books
  for Children, Inc.
1841 Broadway, Rm. 500
New York, NY 10023
212-757-5339

ERIC Clearinghouse on
  Elementary and Early
  Childhood Education (ERIC/
  EECE)
College of Education
University of Illinois
805 W. Pennsylvania Ave.
Urbana, IL 61801-4897
217-333-1386

ERIC Clearinghouse on
  Languages and Linguistics
Center for Applied Linguistics
3520 Prospect St., N.W.
Washington, DC 20007
202-298-9292

ERIC Clearinghouse on
  Reading and
  Communication Skills
National Council of Teachers
  of English
1111 Kenyon Rd.
Urbana, IL 61801
217-328-3870

ERIC Clearinghouse on
  Teacher Education
American Association of
  Colleges for Teacher
  Education
1 Dupont Circle, N.W.
Suite 610
Washington, DC 20036
202-293-2450

Integrated Education
  Association
School of Education
Northwestern University
2003 Sheridan Road
Evanston, IL 60201

National Association for the
  Advancement of Colored
  People
186 Remsen St.
Brooklyn, NY 11201
212-858-0800

National Association for the
  Education of Young
  Children
1834 Connecticut Ave., N.W.
Washington, DC 20009
202-232-8777   800-424-2460

New York Library Association
Children & Young Adult
  Services Section
15 Park Row
Suite 434
New York, NY 10038
212-227-8032

Social Science Education
  Consortium
855 Broadway
Boulder, CO 80302
303-492-8154

References

Almy, M. *The Early Childhood Educator at Work.* New York: McGraw-Hill, 1975.

Banks, J. A. "Evaluating and Selecting Ethnic Studies Materials." *Educational Leadership* 31, no. 7 (April 1974): 593–596.

Banks, J. A. *Teaching Strategies for Ethnic Studies,* 2nd ed. Boston: Allyn & Bacon, 1979.

Boyer, J. *Administrators' Checklist for Enhancing Multi-Cultural Curriculum (Multi-Ethnic, Non-Sexist).* Manhattan, Kan.: College of Education, Kansas State University, n.d. (ERIC Document Reproduction Service No. 135 895).

1976 Curriculum Guidelines for Multiethnic Education, Position Papers. Arlington, Va.: National Council for the Social Studies, 1976.

Dunfee, M. *Report of a Conference on Ethnic Modification of the Curriculum.* Washington, D.C.: Association for Supervision and Curriculum Development, 1969.

Dunfee, M. "Curriculum Materials for Celebrating the Bicentennial." *Educational Leadership* 33, no. 4 (January 1976): 267–272.

Fair Textbooks: A Resource Guide. United States Commission on Civil Rights Clearinghouse Publication 61. Washington, D.C.: U.S. Government Printing Office, (Stock #005-00000224-9) December 1979.

Gold, M. J.; Grant, C. A.; and Rivlin, H. N., eds. *In Praise of Diversity: A Resource Book for Multicultural Education.* Washington, D.C.: Teacher Corps/Association of Teacher Educators, 1977.

Grant, C. A., ed. *Multicultural Education: Commitments, Issues and Applications.* Washington, D.C.: Association for Supervision and Curriculum Development, 1977.

Hirschfelder, A., and Califf, J. "A Thanksgiving Lesson Plan: Celebration or Mourning? It's All in the Point of View." *Council on Interracial Books for Children Bulletin* 10, no. 6 (1979): 6–10.

Jenkins, E. "Greetings in Many Languages. Travellin' with Ella Jenkins." Folkways Records FC 7640. Glendale, Calif.: Bowmar, n.d.

Mussen, P.; Conger, J. J.; and Kagan, J. *Child Development and Personality*, 4th ed. New York: Harper & Row, 1974.

Ramsey, P. "Beyond 'Ten Little Indians' and Turkeys: Alternative Approaches to Thanksgiving." *Young Children* 34, no. 6 (September 1979): 28–32, 49–52.

Spodek, B. *Teaching in the Early Years.* Englewood Cliffs, N.J.: Prentice-Hall, 1978.

Tiedt, P. L., and Tiedt, I. M. *Multicultural Teaching.* Boston: Allyn & Bacon, 1979.

Walsh, H. M. *Introducing the Young Child to the Social World.* New York: Macmillan, 1980.

Williams, J. E., and Morland, K. *Race, Color and the Young Child.* Chapel Hill, N.C.: University of North Carolina Press, 1976.

Wynar, L. R., and Wynar, A. T., eds. *Encylopedic Directory of Ethnic Newspapers and Periodicals in the United States*, 2nd ed. Littleton, Co.: Libraries Unlimited, 1972.

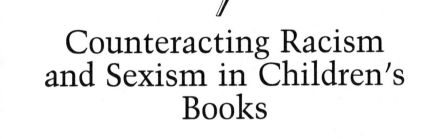

Bradford Chambers

7

Counteracting Racism and Sexism in Children's Books

A stereotype is an oversimplified, generalized image describing all individuals in a group as having the same characteristics, that is to say, in appearance, in behavior, in beliefs. While there may be a germ of truth in a stereotype, the image usually represents a gross distortion, or an exaggeration of that truth, and has offensive, dehumanizing implications. (Council on Interracial Books for Children 1978)

Many stereotypes are concerned with race, sex, age, physical condition, and class. One way they are passed on from generation to generation is through children's books, which reflect and at the same time perpetuate the values of a society. Given a society such as that in the United States that has antihuman values which oppress people of color, women, older people, disabled people, and low-income people, these values will surface in the content of children's books and will thereby be transmitted to successive generations. While there are numerous other ways by which society's values are passed on from one generation to the next, including television, family attitudes, greeting cards, and toys, children's books play a far more important role than is commonly recognized.

Stereotypes serve a function. Stereotypes about women and Third World people are sometimes used to justify their unfair and unjust social, economic, and political treatment. From this perspective, stereotypes serve to rationalize—and to maintain—the status quo.

Young children are the most vulnerable to stereotypes and

bias in books because books play a major role in shaping children's first images of the larger society. These children are forming perceptions of themselves and of others. It is from the content of children's books and the stories told to them that they derive these perceptions. Thus, picture books are critically important. When the all-important initial images are positive, children are likely to develop healthy self-concepts. When these first images are distorted and negative, there is evidence that children's self-images suffer.

Consider the messages transmitted by classic fairy tales. The best known of these are European and reflect cultural and economic values and attitudes of White, Western peoples. Western societies have undergone substantial changes since these tales were recorded but societal values and beliefs have not changed appreciably. By repeating the tales to children at their most impressionable age we reinforce attitudes and values that are, at best, obsolete and, more importantly, in a multicultural society like ours, dysfunctional. Early childhood educators are questioning with greater frequency the socialization process that prepares children for a middle- and upper-class, White male-dominated society. Yet these classic fairy tales remain an extremely important socializing influence.

In addition, fairy tale heroes rely on beauty, good luck, magic, or mysticism to overcome adversity rather than taking action themselves to confront causes of a problem. To convey to young children that beauty (by whose standards?), good luck, or magic will do away with injustice is a severe deterrence to children's learning that action, particularly group action, is essential to overcoming injustice and oppression. Teachers and parents can, however, help children to develop the skills to analyze stereotypes and negative values in stories and thereby immunize them, so to speak, against the worst effects of the content of stories.

While many modern picture books are retellings or newly illustrated versions of older fairy tales, it is also important to look critically at literature that is a product of the society in which we now live.

Sexism in children's literature

The immensely popular *Richard Scarry's Best Word Book Ever* (Scarry 1963) could be titled "The Best Stereotypes Ever."

This and his other picture books transmit messages that prepare a whole new generation to accept rigid sex-role models in the guise of innocent, fun-loving little animals. For example, a double-page spread under *Tools* shows 10 male animals and no females using saws, a hammer, and trowels. The *Toys* spread shows 13 male animals with toys including scooters, trucks, and trains, and 2 female animals—1 with a doll and 1 with a tea set. The *Music Making* section consists of 2 females, 1 at a piano and 1 playing a harp, with 24 other instruments played by males. A section entitled *When You Grow Up* provides females with options to become a nurse, a singer, a dancer, a librarian, a secretary, a teacher, a good cook, or a mommy while males can become—in addition to a daddy—a member of 1 of 20 professions.

Considering the tremendous influence of these books on impressionable young children, one would hope that Scarry's later books might reflect some of the new consciousness sparked by the civil rights and women's movements. His newest books show one concession to the women's movement: he has changed *fireman* to *firefighter*. But his female animals still usually wear dresses or aprons and behave, for the most part, in traditional ways.

The Council on Interracial Books for Children received a letter from Scarry (1977) responding to a group of second-graders who had written him protesting his frequent use of the racially offensive "I is for Indian." The children objected that because Scarry did not use other people to represent letters of the alphabet, only objects, why should he depict an Indian for the letter *i*? The reason Scarry gave in his letter for depicting Indians that way was "I like Indians." This patronizing perspective toward people of color pervades children's literature in our society. The perspective is White, contemptuous of females except in traditional roles, and oriented to the needs of the upper classes. The Scarry books are popular precisely because they mirror--in a skillful manner--our society's dominant values. That children's books both reflect and perpetuate the values of society cannot be emphasized enough.

A picture book useful to explore sex-role stereotyping is *I'm Glad I'm a Boy, I'm Glad I'm a Girl* (Darrow 1970). This is an excellent example of blatant stereotyping, although it is now out of print. In a workshop setting, when extracts of the book are read aloud, they are usually greeted by participants with nervous giggles. As the cruelty of the text increases, the giggles give way to surprised gasps and occasional angry jeers:

Boys are doctors/Girls are nurses.
Boys are football players/Girls are cheerleaders.
Boys invent things/Girls use the things that boys invent.
Boys fix things/Girls need things fixed.
Boys are Presidents/Girls are First Ladies. (p. 22)

This book can easily get a group discussing the way children's books stereotype and distort the image of women.

The Giving Tree (Silverstein 1964) has escalated in popularity in recent years, achieving almost a cult status among college students and young adults. While this is not a picture book, although it appears to be one, *The Giving Tree* contains assumptions about female and male relationships that are also pervasive in books for the very young. The book tells of a young boy's lifelong relationship with a tree. In his youth the boy gathers her leaves, swings in her branches, and eats her apples. As a teenager he carves his valentines in her trunk and lies in her shade with his sweetheart. As he grows older he shuns childish games, although the tree implores him to return. He stays away for longer periods, and returns only when he needs money to buy things, wood for a house, a boat to sail away from it all. In the end as a gnarled old man, he returns looking for a place to rest. Each time he asks the tree for something, she responds by giving him a part of herself--her apples to sell for money, her branches for a home, and finally, her weathered stump for a place to sit and rest. Each time she gives of herself the author tells us "the tree was happy."

By choosing the female pronoun for the all-giving tree and the male pronoun for the all-taking boy, the author projects the prototypical male-female relationship. In this male supremacist's fantasy, we see the idealized traditional relationship of mother/son, wife/husband, mistress/lover. It is no surprise to learn that the author has been a cartoonist for *Playboy*.

One quick way to check out a children's book for sexism is to look at the copyright date which appears on the reverse of the book's title page. Children's books written before the advent of the recent women's movement, around 1970, generally fail to reflect the new consciousness and contain restrictive role models. However, do not rely solely on the copyright date. There are exceptions to this rule.

An outstanding exception is *Mommies at Work* (Merriam 1955). This picture book changed the status quo by showing mothers at work in a wide variety of occupations. It is a wonderful book, and Merriam deserves the plaudits of us all. Some have expressed disappointment that on the last page the author uses a stereotype in telling children that the job all mothers "love best of all [is] to be your very own mommy, and coming home to *you!*"

Racism in children's literature

Little Black Sambo (Bannerman n.d.) has been around for more than three-quarters of a century. As the awareness of racism has grown in recent years, it has been the topic of extensive debate. When it first appeared in 1898, the intent was innocent enough; indeed, *Little Black Sambo* introduced a new format and style. It was the first book of a size children could easily hold in their hands, and it did much to innovate nonsense humor, repetitive cadence, and rhythm in writing for children. The problem is that *Little Black Sambo* reflects the strong derogatory stereotype Whites held about Black people at the time it was written and illustrated. While Black people have long regarded the book as offensive, many Whites refuse to accept their protest.

The name *Sambo* is itself offensive. From the very beginning of the Black experience in the United States, the term was used interchangeably with *slave*. Later, during the period of the minstrel shows, Sambo was the black-faced, thick-red-lipped stupid character, the butt of all the jokes. By the mid-nineteenth century, the term was used to refer to any Black person, almost always with derision and contempt, and throughout the midtwentieth century, as a nickname to call porters and shoeshiners.

Birtha, a Black librarian, makes the following comment (1969):

> The argument has been offered, children don't know or care about the background of a name. They only listen to the story. But it has been proved—and experienced—that if a story of this type is used in an integrated story hour or classroom, there is a certain amount of discomfort and even, yet, inferiority feeling—for a black child when white classmates look at him and giggle, later teasing him by calling him Sambo. No matter how entertaining a book may be, one group of children should never be entertained at the expense of another group's feelings. (p. 190)

The illustrations in this book are also offensive. They depict Black people with exaggerated, grotesque features and large, protruding lips, dressed in minstrel clothes of clashing colors topped with a green umbrella, and having inordinate appetites. This was the popular image of black people at the time Bannerman, a White British woman whose husband was a surgeon stationed in India, wrote the story. To this day the image fits into and reinforces the perceptions White chauvinists hold about Black people.

In addition, the theme is offensive. In the story, the Black child is saved in the end, not through his own accomplishments but because of the cupidity and avariciousness of the tigers. Compare this with another story by Bannerman (1966), *Little White Squibba*, one of the eight books she wrote and illustrated all in the same format. In *Little White Squibba*, a White child—the only White child in the series—appears in a forest, too, and is faced with perils. At the story's end, however, the White child is saved by her own wit.

The perspective of White authors that endows a White child with wit and intelligence but not a Black child constitutes a fundamental stereotype in children's literature and continues to plague books by White authors to this day.

The picture book *The Five Chinese Brothers* (Bishop 1938) is to Asian Americans what *Little Black Sambo* is to Blacks: a blatant symbol of cultural racism. *The Five Chinese Brothers*, illustrated by Kurt Wiese, has been one of the most widely circulated children's books in the United States until recently. It can be found in many early childhood programs, and when non-Asian parents ask librarians for a children's book about Asian people, librarians almost always give them *The Five Chinese Brothers*.

It is a skillfully done book, capturing and holding young people's attention. But is the appeal of a picture book to children sufficient reason to recommend its use? We think not. There is the flagrant stereotype of all Asians looking alike in this book. Not only the five brothers but *all* the characters—the townspeople, the judge, the mother—all are identical in appearance. Moreover, the characters are reduced to the common stereotypical denominator of bilious yellow skin, slitted and slanted eyes, queues, and *coolie* clothes. Asian people's skin is *not* yellow, and their eyes are neither slanted nor slitted. Caricatures like these reflect the historical perception of Asians held by White Westerners, a preception that has led members of the White majority to persecute, ridicule, exploit, and ostracize Asian Americans.

The origins of certain details of the stereotypes in *The Five Chinese Brothers* and their sociopolitical significance are noteworthy. The queue was a humiliating symbol of subjugation forced upon Chinese peasants by the Manchu ruling class. In the United States, during the Manchu reign in China, White Americans often frightened and humiliated Chinese Americans by cutting off their queues, knowing that they could not return to China, should they want to, without the queues. When the Manchus were overthrown in 1911, the Chinese cut off their queues as an act of liberation and adopted new hair styles. For an illustrator in 1937 to portray Chinese people with queues reflects gross insensitivity. The characters' *coolie* clothes are also associated with subjugation.

Criticizing stereotypes in *The Five Chinese Brothers* invites the charge that a mountain is being made out of a molehill. Why take the book so seriously? It was not intended as a historically accurative narrative; it was meant to be humorous and entertaining—a tall tale of sorts. That may well be, but one is hard put to divorce such a book from the tradition of racism which Asians have had to suffer in American society or from the specific manifestations of that racism which surfaced during the period in which the book was written. The Asian images presented in the book coincide with and strongly reinforce—intentionally or otherwise—the negative perceptions of Asians that are still held operative in our society. It is important to realize that such perceptions have also informed our foreign policy toward Asian nations.

Studies of children's books

An instance of racist and sexist stereotyping or bias in a book here and there is serious in itself; even more serious is the constant repetition of stereotyping in many books. The first instance reveals the prejudice or ignorance of an individual author; the second indicates a prevailing cultural attitude or bias. Over the years the Council on Interracial Books for Children (CIBC) has undertaken a number of comprehensive studies, analyzing all the children's books available about different minority groups. What follows is a summary of two of these studies: one of books on Puerto Rican, the other on Asian-American themes.

All children's books about minority groups are reviewed for the CIBC by members of that particular minority. Thus, a book about Blacks is evaluated by a Black reviewer, and a book about Chicanos is evaluated by a Chicano reviewer. The CIBC feels that a person from a particular culture will give a more sensitive and authentic evaluation than a person not from that culture, particularly for groups that have been oppressed by White society. Most children's book authors are from that group and therefore have a very different perspective from members of the minority culture. While this procedure *does not* guarantee the authenticity of the review, it is likely to result in more authentic, more informative reviews.

The first comprehensive CIBC study of all the children's books available about a minority group involved Puerto Ricans (CIBC 1976). Excerpts from the study appear below:

> In conforming to today's demand for "socially relevant" books, publishers and writers have generated a new genre of books dealing with "The Puerto Rican Problem." The result has been books with a theme but no content, with a Ghetto, U.S.A., background but without memorable characters—and what in other books would be the setting has, in these books, become the story. The story lines are marked by a virtual absence of humor, and the characters are portrayed as having a poverty of emotion or inner fantasy life—in brief, the stories are decidedly lacking in literary merit.
>
> This is not to deny the need for books that deal with the realities of urban ghetto life. But when books about Puerto Ricans present *nothing but* this single topic, then the books become racist rather than relevant. For what they say is that the only possible reality for a Puerto Rican must be a poverty-stricken ghetto existence.
>
> On top of this is the pervasive political bias of the authors. Ghetto problems are portrayed as inherent to Puerto Ricans. For the resolution of problems, the authors place the onus on the Puerto Ricans, not on where the blame belongs—the racist practices of U.S. society. . . .
>
> The Puerto Rican image endlessly repeated in the books is this. From an idyllic farm in Puerto Rico—always a beautiful gentle, *small* island—emerges a family that is happy or unconcerned about their country's dependent status on the U.S. The family moves to New York, either to make money, or for no apparent reason. They move in the cold of winter (Puerto Ricans never seem to make the trip to New York in spring, summer, or fall).

Once settled in a run-down and badly overcrowded apartment in the inner-city ghetto, the family begins the task of "adjusting." In the picture books and early childhood readers, the adjustment follows a simplistic pattern, repeated over and over again. A young child is troubled by an inability to speak English and by loneliness for Puerto Rico and friends left behind. These troubles disappear as soon as the child (a) learns some words in English, (b) makes a friend, (c) is given a doll or a pet, or finds a lost one, or (d) sees her/his first snowfall. These events became solutions, or rather, very pat devices that instantly transform the troubled child into a happy, laughing one—and the story ends. (p. 14)

The magic formula of the picture books becomes more complex in books for older children, but the devices used to resolve the conflicts are equally pat—in the older books there are plenty of problems and these are always solved by the beneficence of a White social worker, never a Puerto Rican social worker, or by a White minister or church leader, never a Puerto Rican leader. Of course, disbelief in the ability of Third World people to solve their problems is the very nub of racism.

Of the 100 children's books reviewed in the *Interracial Books for Children Bulletin*, 94 of them were authored by White middle-class writers, a great many of whom live in the suburbs, far removed from the realities of urban life. Thus, besides the distortions already noted, the books are flawed by gross inaccuracies deriving from confusion about Puerto Rican traditions and customs—and from misconceptions of what it is to live in the ghetto.

—Law enforcers are depicted as the people's best friend. This may be true in middle-class neighborhoods, where the authors live but is contrary to reality in the ghetto.

—Teachers are portrayed as loving, kind, bilingual, and as having answers to all problems. Such is not reality in New York City schools, the setting of almost all the stories.

—Contrived and stilted English is used as a device to suggest that a foreigner is speaking. Short, simple sentences, verbs always in the present tense, and absence of contractions may be among speech patterns that non-Puerto Rican writers *think* Puerto Ricans use but this is erroneous and highly offensive.

—Puerto Rican names in the books are often Italian rather than Spanish—Carlo mistaken for Carlos, Carlotta mistaken for Carlota, for example.

—Mexican customs, dress, and foods are erroneously used as if they were Puerto Rican.

—Notably lacking in the books are Puerto Ricans of African descent, or Afro-Borinquens. This not only ignores the significant African contribution to Puerto Rican culture but falsifies the reality of the Puerto Rican racial makeup.

Of the 100 books reviewed, not 1 could be found that the reviewers—scholars and instructors in Puerto Rican Studies departments of universities in the New York area—felt could be unreservedly recommended. So that at least some books might be recommended, the reviewers selected 10 that they regarded as the *least offensive* books. One publisher actually used this as a commendation for *Angelita* (Kesselman and Holt 1970): "One of the ten books," stated *The New York Times* ad, "to be selected by Council reviewers as the least offensive."

A second comprehensive study was undertaken by the Asian American Children's Book Project to identify books currently in print depicting Asian Americans and to analyze the books for accuracy and authenticity. To evaluate Asian-American children's books, members of the project approached an organization active in fighting discrimination in New York's Chinatown called *The Basement Workshop*.

Although the term *Asian American* technically includes Americans of all Asian, including East Indian, Southeast Asian, and Pacific, backgrounds, the reviewers limited their analyses to books about Chinese, Japanese, Korean, and Vietnamese Americans. They identified a total of 66 such books, published between 1945 and 1975, with the greatest number appearing in the early 1970s (CIBC 1976).

The major conclusion was that, with one or perhaps two exceptions, the 66 books are

> racist, sexist and elitist, and the image of Asian Americans they represent is grossly misleading. A succinct definition of the image presented in children's books would be: Asian Americans are foreigners who all look alike and who choose to live together in quaint communities in the midst of large cities and who cling to "outworn," alien customs. Problems with the books found by the Council reviewers were these:
>
> First, the books misrepresent Asian American cultures, emphasizing exotic festivals, ancient superstitions and costumes and, by contrast (stated or unstated), boost the American Way of Life.
>
> Second, the books promote the myth of Asian Americans as a "model minority," with the myth serving as a smokescreen to conceal the realities of white racism. The "model minority" myth also serves as a divisive tactic to effectively alienate "hard-work-

ing" Asian Americans from other minorities by implying that the latter, too, would "make it" if they only worked harder.

Third, the books give the misleading notion that hard work, education (in particular, learning to speak English correctly) and a low profile will overcome adversity and necessarily lead to success.

And fourth, the books measure success by the extent to which Asian Americans have assimilated white middle-class attitudes and values. (Adapted from p. 3)

As in other CIBC studies, the project found that far too many children's books defining a Third World experience are written by Whites. Of the 66 books evaluated, only 11 were written by 7 authors of Asian-American background. Asian-American authors constituted one-sixth of all the authors.

The CIBC has also published a special issue of the *Interracial Books for Children Bulletin* (CIBC 1975) devoted to a multicultural perspective of day care and early childhood education. In the preparation of that issue books published for young children were examined to identify those that fit the following criteria:

■ portray people in nonstereotyped ways with regard to race, sex, and age
■ project to children culturally authentic images of different peoples
■ build in *all* children respect for Third World peoples
■ encourage among children new values and priorities for a society free from racism, sexism, ageism, and classism (Vol. 6, nos. 5 and 6, p. 9)

Not a single picture book reviewed met all these criteria. Some books were free of sexist stereotypes but contained racist elements and some books were free of racist stereotypes but contained sexism. The CIBC also found some books authentic in their presentation of one Third World group but unwittingly demeaning toward another. The CIBC was able to recommend 20 books on African-American themes; 6 books on Asian-American themes; no books on Chicano themes; 4 books on Native-American themes; 8 books on Puerto Rican themes; and 8 books that presented young girls in a positive image and at the same time did not demean any child. That is an extraordinarily small number of books. Some very positive books for preschool children have appeared in the years since this special *Interracial Books for Children Bulletin* issue on day care and early childhood education appeared. But there is still a shockingly small number of books that meet the needs of children growing up in a multicultural society—books that will help children become bias-free adults.

Counteracting racism and sexism in children's books

How can we counteract racism and sexism in children's books? A first step is for all of us to become aware of how bias is manifested in books and to develop the skills to recognize and identify stereotypes. One way to develop these skills is through teacher education and in-service training programs for early childhood educators.

A second but critical step is to make certain that children's books we offer as parents and teachers are free of racist and sexist content. Simple as this sounds, it is a highly sensitive, complicated task. Who is to determine which books are biased and which are bias free? For many of us, our own socialization in a racist and sexist society has hindered our perceptions, and all too frequently we overlook stereotypes, especially the subtle, covert ones.

We at CIBC have learned that the most effective way to recognize racist and other biased content is by consulting people who both belong to oppressed groups and who are active in the fight to overcome their oppression. Third World activists, feminists, disabled and older people active in antidiscrimination struggles—these are the individuals who possess the insights and sensitivity so important to a valid selection process.

Essential, too, are criteria and guidelines—and training in their use—so that people who select new books and reevaluate old ones will approach their task from an informed and critical position. At the suggestion of the U.S. Office of Education, the CIBC compiled all the criteria and guidelines prepared by CIBC task forces during the past 15 years in *Guidelines for Selecting Bias-Free Textbooks and Storybooks* (CIBC 1980). These guidelines were prepared by task forces consisting of racial minorities, feminists, disability rights activists, all providing the perspectives that have traditionally been missing in review media. The manual is a useful tool for early childhood educators, yet we encourage groups whenever possible to develop their own guidelines—working jointly, of course, with minorities and feminists.

It is important that we make a distinction between children's books that are racist, nonracist, and antiracist and children's books that are sexist, nonsexist, and antisexist. Racist and sexist books, of course, contain stereotypes and thereby perpetuate racism and sexism. Nonracist or nonsexist children's books do not contain stereotypes. However, books may be free of stereotypes and still not contribute to the elimination of racism and sexism. Such books are referred to as neutral books. While these are preferred to racist or sexist books, by being neutral and not taking a stand, they support the status quo. An avowedly antiracist or antisexist children's book is one that takes a conscious stand against racism and sexism and gives a positive message.

How do we get authors to write antiracist, antisexist books and then how do we get those books published? Children's books cannot be written by formula. We do the cause of children's literature an injustice if, in seeking new books, we fail to take into account the interplay of skills and talent required to create children's books.

Most established authors seem to lack the requisite antiracist, antisexist awareness. They continue to write on the themes with which they are most at east. Publishers are not going to encourage their authors to write on themes other than those that now sell. The unfortunate reality of the marketplace is that books with stereotypes *are* popular. After all, if you believe—as we at the CIBC believe—that books reflect the values of society, then the popular books will be those that best reflect society's values. That is just what is happening— racist and sexist children's books are the books that sell.

Of course, there are small presses but children's books with appealing multicolor reproductions are expensive to produce, and these presses just don't have the resources to print multicolored picture books. We have seen small presses publish low-cost books with the best of intentions only to have the product marred by uninspired writing that lacks quality and/ or by unattractive art.

How can we develop writers with the talent and skills to create antiracist, antisexist children's books? How can we develop networks for publishing and disseminating the materials once they have been created? If we cannot rely on the commercial publishers or small presses and if we must go beyond the established channels for recruiting writers of children's books, then we need to start looking for other creative ways.

Perhaps the answers can be found in our local communities. Perhaps we can develop community-based publishing programs with funding from foundations and community agencies. Perhaps we can help children write their own books. While we don't have the answers, we can at least start asking the questions.

For too long we have thought of children's picture books as amusing little objects, perhaps helpful in teaching letters of the alphabet, numbers, and other concepts. It is time we started to consider the values that are transmitted through these books. When we see a children's book, let our immediate response be to stop, look, and ask: "What is that book saying to a child? Are there stereotypes in the content of the book? What are the book's hidden messages?"

It may not seem fair to burden our early childhood teachers with yet another task. But who else will take the responsibility for selecting and encouraging the creation of children's books that give positive images to all children and that will take a stand against racism and sexism? If not us, who else will shoulder the task?

References

Bannerman, H. *Little Black Sambo*. New York: Platt & Munk, n.d.

Bannerman, H. *Little White Squibba*. London: Chatto & Windus, 1966. Published posthumously in England; not published in the United States.

Birtha, J. J. "Portrayal of the Black in Children's Literature." *Pennsylvania Library Association Bulletin* 24 (July 1969).

Bishop, C. H. *The Five Chinese Brothers*. New York: Coward, McCann & Geoghegan, 1938.

Council on Interracial Books for Children. "Feminists Look at the 100 Books." *Interracial Books for Children Bulletin* 4, nos. 1 and 2 (1972a): 7–10.

Council on Interracial Books for Children. "100 Children's Books about Puerto Ricans: A Study in Racism, Sexism and Colonialism." *Interracial Books for Children Bulletin* 4, nos. 1 and 2 (1972b): 1, 14–15. A 10-year update of the 1972 analysis is in press and will be available in the *Interracial Books for Children Bulletin* 14, nos. 1 and 2.

Council on Interracial Books for Children. "Toward a Multicultural Collection: Recommended Picture Books for Young Children." *Interracial Books for Children Bulletin* 6, nos. 5 and 6 (1975): 1–20.

Council on Interracial Books for Children. "How Children's Books

Distort the Asian American Image." *Interracial Books for Children Bulletin* 7, nos. 2 and 3 (1976): 2–23.

Council on Interracial Books for Children. "Identifying Racism and Sexism in Children's Books." (filmstrip) New York: Racism and Sexism Resource Center for Educators, 1978.

Council on Interracial Books for Children. *Guidelines for Selecting Bias-Free Textbooks and Storybooks.* New York: CIBC, 1980.

Darrow, W., Jr. *I'm Glad I'm a Boy, I'm Glad I'm a Girl.* New York: Simon & Schuster, 1970.

Kesselman, W., and Holt, N. *Angelita.* New York: Hill & Wang, 1970.

Merriam, E. *Mommies at Work.* New York: Knopf, 1955.

Scarry, R. *Richard Scarry's Best Word Book Ever.* New York: Golden, 1963.

Scarry, R. Written correspondence. 1977.

Silverstein, S. *The Giving Tree.* New York: Harper & Row, 1964.

The Council on Interracial Books for Children has produced the following training filmstrips for early childhood educators: "Unlearning Asian American Stereotypes," "Unlearning 'Indian' Stereotypes," and "Unlearning Chicano and Puerto Rican Stereotypes." CIBC has also produced two additional filmstrips of relevance to early childhood educators: "Childcare Shapes the Future: Anti-Racist Strategies" and "Childcare Shapes the Future: Anti-Sexist Strategies." A free catalog of consciousness-raising materials is available from CIBC, 1841 Broadway, New York, NY 10023.

Theresa Herrera Escobedo

Parent and Community Involvement:

A Blueprint for a Successful Program

Parents have always been responsible for the education of their children, an education that has included the transmission of moral and social knowledge as well as practical skills for making a livelihood. The ancient Greek government was greatly concerned with the education of the young, they believed in the joint responsibility of parents and the state in rearing children (Berger 1981; Braun and Edwards 1972). Religious implications are also attached to parents' roles as educators, as demonstrated by Massachusetts laws of 1642, 1643, and 1647, which made parents responsible for the education of their children as a means of salvation. Some present day educators emphasize that if parents have the obligation to teach children, then schools have the responsibility to help parents learn how to teach effectively.

At times, such as during the 1950s in the United States, parents were viewed as interfering observers in the education of their own children. However, during the 1960s, parents were again considered to have an important socializing influence on their children, as programs for special needs or low-SES children were more effective when parents were involved. In addition, other children in the family as well as the target child seemed to benefit from parent involvement (Bronfenbrenner 1974). Many of these children were from socially and culturally different backgrounds. Thus, it is apparent that the need to prepare educators to work effectively with parents is particularly acute for teachers who work in multicultural settings.

The guidelines for many federally funded educational programs for young children require that parents be involved in various activities ranging from teacher home visits to parent advisory groups. Interactions between school and home may be new to parents and teachers, necessitating carefully planned programs to ensure the smooth execution of activities. An approach to the development of a parent and community involvement program should include strategies for cooperation in goal setting, planning, and implementation. These strategies can help teachers and other school personnel in multicultural settings to enhance interactions with parents that will benefit children.

Establishing goals for parent programs

Although educators concur that parent-community involvement is beneficial, they disagree on how parent programs can best be implemented. In addition, parents and teachers may be reluctant to cooperate because of fear or awe of one another and because of lack of knowledge and experience with home-school relations. These fears are multiplied when teachers and parents come from different cultural and linguistic backgrounds (Escobedo 1979). In order to alleviate these problems, the first step in establishing a program is to assess school, parent, and community needs, taking into account socioeconomic status and cultural background so as to develop realistic goals. This assessment can also help in determining the level of involvement that is feasible and the dimensions of the program that are desirable to ultimately realize the established goals.

Various authors have defined parent involvement, its various components, and its levels of involvement; this may be helpful in planning and establishing goals for parent programs. According to Bauch, Vietze, and Morris (1973), parent programs may include:

A. Parental participation aimed exclusively at assisting the parents in their role as educational facilitator for their child. . . .
B. Parental participation with mutual benefit to parents and to the early education program
C. Parental participation in support of the early education program (pp. 47–53)

The goal of the first approach is to improve parenting skills through workshops on subjects such as child growth and development. The second approach trains parents for paid jobs such as teacher aids while they serve as resources to the children's program. The third provides opportunities for parents to serve as volunteers to supplement the paid staff of a school.

Scriven (1975) categorizes parent involvement into three levels:

1. Enhancement of communication through parent conferences and parent meetings
2. Involvement of parents in the instructional program as resources and volunteers
3. Involvement of parents in policy and curriculum decisions (pp. 53–56)

All three levels of participation are seen as essential in a school program in order to improve parent-teacher relations. Gordon (1970) and Gordon and Breivogel (1976) further delineate levels to identify five different levels of parent involvement:

- audience or bystander-observer
- teacher of the child
- volunteer
- trained worker
- participant in decision-making (p. 7)

Traditionally most attempts at parent involvement have been at the first level (Greenwood, Breivogel, and Bessent 1972). Today, however, many parent involvement programs include parent advisory councils or committees, although opportunities for true decision making by parents may still be limited (Rodriguez 1980). This may be especially true for minority parents on councils which are established as a formality to fulfill a requirement.

Lillie (1975) describes four dimensions essential to the development of parent programs:

1. Providing social and emotional support
2. Exchanging information with parents
3. Improving parent-child interactions
4. Parent participation (p. 193)

Social and emotional support promotes a positive attitude in parents about their role as teachers of their own children and also enhances their personal self-concepts. The exchange of information between parents and teachers is essential for each to gain an understanding of the child's continuous growth and development both at home and at school. In addition, this exchange of information provides parents with information about objectives of the program and provides teachers with better understanding of the child's home life. Lillie maintains that parent programs should offer opportunities for parents to stimulate their children's cognitive, emotional, and social development.

All four of these dimensions are important in working with culturally different parents who have traditionally been excluded from mainstream education. This exclusion has, in many cases, caused parents to be reluctant to approach schools to find out about their child's program, to exchange information, or to become involved as volunteers. Language barriers and feelings of insecurity or low self-esteem also have been cited as factors contributing to this reluctance.

Because teachers are for the most part responsible for implementing parent involvement activities, it is important that their needs also be considered in planning a parent program. Successful implementation of the program depends on the type of interactions that occur between teachers and parents. Therefore, parent programs should include training to improve teachers' skills in communicating and working effectively with parents (Nedler and McAfee 1979).

Perhaps the greatest difficulty for school personnel lies in developing attitudes toward parents as co-workers. These attitudes are vital in order to encourage parents to participate in decision making. Parents are often viewed as a threat or as incompetent to make decisions regarding curriculum and teaching approaches. Sessions designed to support positive attitudes on the part of both parents and teachers can do much to establish a parent program on a solid basis. Clarification of roles and expectations that parents and teachers have for each other may be accomplished through carefully guided group discussions with opportunities for interaction. An early concern for the development of positive attitudes will increase cooperation in later activities (Croft 1979).

Components of parent programs

Parent involvement programs can be seen as having three

major components that can serve as categories to develop the needs assessment and the program plan:

■ Parent involvement in the child's educational activities at home and at school

■ Parent education that will benefit the parents directly

■ Parenting education for training parents to become better parents

These components can be further subdivided into various degrees of involvement, ranging from noninterfering observers to partners in decision making.

The following outline incorporates the components for a parent program and indicates the degrees of involvement required. This model can be modified to incorporate the needs of each particular community.

I. Initial contact with parents (necessary for all subsequent components)
   A. Communication and recruitment regarding all components and/or activities
      1. News media—radio, television, newspaper announcements
      2. Notices, letters, and newsletters
      3. Personal contact, phone calls, home visits
   B. Orientation to parent program
      1. Meetings at school for tours, programs of interest (for example, multicultural films), or other activities
      2. Get-acquainted socials in each classroom
      3. Coffee lounge (use of teachers' lounge for parent coffee once a week or monthly)
      4. Individual contact at school or home
II. Parent education
   A. School related
      1. Meetings and/or communication to share information on parent program
      2. Classroom visits and/or communication to orient parents to classroom activities, curriculum, and other program components
      3. Parent workshops to enhance teaching skills, materials development, and other areas of contribution
   B. Community/survival related
      1. Meetings and/or communication regarding community medical, health, and nutrition services

    2. Information on community entertainment, recreation facilities, cultural events

    3. Continuing education programs

    4. Other topics of interest such as consumer information, budgeting, self-help groups, community participation

III. Parenting education

  A. Child development classes

  B. Training sessions on the care of children

  C. Other sessions to increase parenting skills in areas such as discipline

IV. Parent involvement

  A. Home-based activities

    1. Meetings in neighborhood homes for orientation and/or recruitment

    2. Activities workshops in neighborhood homes to develop teaching games, teaching skills, and other methods of implementation

    3. Home visits to work with parents' child care and teaching skills

  B. School-based activities

    1. Attendance at school meetings

    2. Visits to classroom and occasional participation in classroom activities

  C. Leadership and participation in policy and decision making

    1. Parent leader at meetings

    2. Members or officers of parent advisory group

    3. Involvement and input regarding curriculum, teaching methods, and other areas of education

V. Volunteer aid program—parents and community members

  A. Volunteer orientation

    1. Role of teacher and volunteer

    2. Time commitments and expectations from teacher and volunteer

    3. Professionalism and confidentiality issues

  B. Volunteer training

    1. Observation: classroom arrangement, grouping, activities, behavior management

    2. Materials development, for example, teaching aids, letter painting

    3. Practice in operating machines such as projectors

    4. Supervision of play, field trips, lunch time, and other events

     5. Volunteer tutor to work directly with children in different content areas such as language activities or math

  C. Volunteer organization

     1. Coordinator of volunteer activities (paid position if possible)

     2. Clerical assistance to coordinator including, for example, scheduling volunteer hours

     3. School-community liaison

Implementation strategies

The remainder of this chapter will focus on involvement of parents in their child's education and on the skills that teachers need in order to implement parent program activities. Teachers generally have limited training in the area of working with parents. Even when students take college courses in this area, they find it difficult to have the necessary practical experiences. Most teachers who are successful in parent involvement learn by trial and error. Several basic interaction skills and attitudes can be identified including communication that imparts acceptance of parents and sensitivity to individual needs and differences. These are probably even more important when teachers and parents come from different cultures and socio-economic backgrounds.

Teachers need to know about the school community (Berger 1981). If language differences create barriers between teachers and parents, a bilingual parent can serve as community liaison and interpreter. Parents can also be invaluable in providing insight into the community. While cultural differences affecting value systems may not be as obvious as language differences, they can be almost as formidable a barrier to mutual understanding (Escobedo 1983). Helping teachers to develop sensitivity in dealing with these differences can ensure that parent-teacher interactions proceed smoothly. Such awareness would also help teachers to recognize that discontinuities in areas other than language may exist between home and school that may hinder the progress of culturally different children in school (Laosa 1977).

Effective communication with parents cannot be stressed enough as the most important step in parent involvement. When the benefits of their involvement are emphasized, parents feel that they are contributing to the school and are more likely to engage in the parent program activities. The following tips from Croft (1979) can be used to communicate to parents the teachers' desire to include them in their child's education and the need for their participation:

■ Provide research information indicating the value of parent involvement

■ Express recognition and appreciation of even the smallest contribution. Praise parents and encourage them to try new tasks they may find enjoyable. Make general announcements about program needs but also ask individuals to do specific tasks at which they excel.

■ Provide opportunities that allow parents to be "experts." Provide options so that parents can work at home or school at tasks that they like to do.

■ Communicate positive comments about their children to parents by phone during times when they are at home or send "happy notes" home with the children.

■ Convince parents that their children will benefit directly from their participation; use every opportunity to build trust and open communications

■ Never criticize or correct a parent in front of others.

■ Interpret clearly the needs of the program and show parents how their involvement can be of real help. (pp. 13–15)

While parents can be helpful to teachers in implementing school-based activities, the time required to recruit and train parents to help in the classroom often keeps teachers from utilizing this valuable resource. Sometimes teachers do not feel comfortable with a parent in the room, and parents may also feel that they are intruding. A well-organized parent participation program will include plans to provide release time for teachers to recruit and train parents or to employ a parent coordinator for these responsibilities. If neither is possible, willing teachers can still include parents by starting with simple activities such as having parents visit the classroom and later showing them how to develop easy-to-make teaching materials. The tasks involved and the training required can be increased gradually so that parents will soon be able to supervise children at the library corner or the art area. Such classroom involvement is even more important for parents from culturally different backgrounds. Their presence creates a link to the home and community that provides a continuity, in the classroom, of what the child knows. This is particularly necessary when the home language is other than English; bilingual parents can provide monolingual English teachers a means of communicating with non-English speaking children. These parents can also contribute cultural information that will be useful to teachers (Escobedo 1979).

A few additional strategies that can help teachers in working with parents in the classroom follow. It is important to remember that expectations should be made clear regarding time commitments and duties. A simple set of guidelines can be developed by the teacher, possibly using suggestions from parents as well.

An efficient way to specify tasks and instructions is to develop a file of activities for parents consisting of a set of activity packages, each with clear instructions on a card and the materials needed for the activity. Activity packages, filed in envelopes, can include matching games, instructions on how to set up the painting easel, directions on where the needed materials are kept, and other simple teaching procedures. The envelopes should be large enough to contain the instruction cards and a list of all needed materials. Go through the packets you expect to use with parents beforehand. On the days that a parent is to be in the classroom, pull out the desired envelope, attach a list of the children who are to participate with the time and area designated, and present them to the parent or leave them in a previously designated place.

Although teachers may not be part of an organized parent program, individual teachers can initiate efforts to involve their parents by extending their own classroom activities. Parents are a teacher's most important resource in reinforcing what teachers want the children to learn, and the teacher's task is made easier when the designated learning continues at home. Guidance from teachers, classroom observation, and participation helps parents develop the teaching skills needed to help their children learn.

Parent conferences—formal and informal—are always a part of teachers' interactions with parents. These may be planned by teachers or initiated by parents because of concern about their child. Much information can be exchanged during informal conversations. However, when teachers plan and initiate the conference, they can determine ahead of time what information should be elicited from or given to the parent and needed materials can be made available (Croft 1979). Some basic steps to help teachers in conducting their parent conference include:

I. Planning and preparing for conference
  A. Plans
    1. Plan at least two conferences a year, the first one as early as possible after the child is enrolled.
    2. Include both parents, if possible.
    3. Allow for extra conferences that may be requested by parents.
  B. Arrangements
    1. Contact parents in person or by telephone.
    2. Send forms home to be filled out and returned stating date and time for the conference. Set time limit.
    3. Arrange for room.
  C. Preparation
    1. Make a folder for each child's work; include a checklist that indicates progress.
    2. Make note of pertinent information or facts to be discussed.
    3. Become familiar with family background.
  D. Setting
    1. Ensure privacy and eliminate possible disruptions.
    2. Provide comfortable seating arrangements and sit beside parent, not behind a desk or table.
    3. Establish an informal, friendly atmosphere.
II. The conference
  A. Social and emotional considerations
    1. Do not either overdress or dress too casually.
    2. Establish rapport—be friendly; do a little social visiting.
    3. Encourage parents to talk but do not insist as some parents may be shy or frightened.
    4. Listen attentively—do not look away, move papers about, or interrupt.
    5. Remember that facial expression and general impressions may impart negative feelings.
  B. Professional considerations
    1. Develop an attitude of cooperation.
    2. Speak in terms parents can understand without being patronizing.
    3. Emphasize the positive aspects of the child's progress and discuss problem areas after rapport has been established.
    4. Encourage suggestions from parents.

      5. Use parents' suggestions in planning for action.

      6. Summarize the points covered.

      7. End on a positive, cooperative note.

  C. Follow up

      1. Make notes *after* the parent leaves unless there is a form to be filled out by the parent.

      2. Keep a record of the conference in the child's folder.

      3. Make notations of helpful insights or suggestions.

      4. Avoid recording any unnecessary confidential or embarrassing information.

      5. *Keep all records confidential.*

III. Important considerations in conferences

  A. Cultural and social considerations

      1. Note which cultural background parents identify with, and the terminology they prefer, for example, Chicano or Mexican American.

      2. Are both parents of the same background and, if not, how does it affect their child?

      3. What languages do they speak? How comfortable do they feel in English?

  B. Educational considerations

      1. Would they be able to read notices sent by you?

      2. In what language should notices be written?

  C. Economic considerations

      1. Do both parents work and what are the hours?

      2. When would be a convenient time for them to come to a conference?

      3. Can they afford to take off work?

      4. Is transportation a problem? Would it be better to go to them instead?

IV. Family considerations

  A. Family structure

      1. Is this a one-parent family?

      2. How many other children are in the family?

      3. Are there other members (extended family) living in the household?

      4. Are there younger children who will need to be cared for during the conference?

  B. Other problems

      1. Will an interpreter be needed?

      2. Is the child having problems that the parents are unaware of?

      3. Would a home visit be more convenient for the par-

ent because of transportation and babysitting problems?

When factors make it difficult for parents to come to a conference at school, a home conference may be needed. Some
federally funded programs, in fact, require that teachers visit
the home to increase parents' involvement. Home visits are
often difficult to implement because of the additional time
required of teachers and the difficulty of providing teachers
released time during the day for visits. If home visits are necessary, teachers should be compensated for the time involved
in after-hour visits. The added support of a community liaison
person might be made available to accompany a teacher who
is not familiar with the neighborhood to minimize anxiety
about going into new or unfamiliar areas. In multicultural situations this liaison person can interpret if necessary and can
help the teacher accommodate cultural differences.

The home visit is one of the best vehicles that teachers can
use to improve understanding and communication. Teachers
can gain insight into home conditions that influence the child
and at the same time gain the parents' trust and cooperation
in the educational process. The visit gives the parents an opportunity to ask questions about the school program and to
learn about activities in which they can participate. The mutual sharing of information about the child may be used in
evaluating progress and planning future goals. Following are
some suggestions for home visits:

■ Prepare a folder or index file that includes the child's
name, birth date, and address and telephone number at home;
both parents' names, occupations, business phones and addresses, and working hours; and the teacher's name.

■ Make arrangements ahead of time. Speak to parents personally to arrange the visit if they bring the child to school.
Otherwise, telephone or mail a note because notes sent with
the child often get lost or are regarded as less important than
regular mail. If sending a note, use stationery or colored paper
with some type of design. Parents are more likely to read a note
if it appears personal and important.

■ Schedule the visit at the parents' convenience. If parents
work, the visit may necessarily be in the evening. Teachers
should be given time off to make up for the time spent.

■ Suggest dates when you will be in the neighborhood if the
parents are undecided as to the date.

■ Be sure parents know why you are visiting. Parents may feel that a teacher's home visits are an invasion of their privacy or associate it with a negative situation in the school.

■ Be sure everyone is aware of the date and time. It is useful to have the parents fill in the date and time on a note and have it returned to the teacher. State on the note that you wish to be notified if anything comes up at the last minute and the parent is unable to be at home at the scheduled time.

■ If parents are unavailable at the time you make the scheduled visit, leave a note saying you will visit at another time.

■ Do not overdress, but do not be so casual in dress or speech that parents will be offended.

■ Use terms familiar to parents to make sure they understand what you are saying but be careful that you do not talk to them in a patronizing way.

■ Do not stare at surroundings as it may indicate criticism to parents. Do not ask questions that may be interpreted as prying.

■ Take refreshments if they are offered. The family may have worked hard to prepare them for you.

■ Discuss something positive about the child.

■ Visit with the child. Contacts between home and school are especially important to a child. Talk to the other children or family members present.

■ Invite the parents to visit the classroom or to observe or participate in the activities.

■ Explain briefly what the class is studying at the particular time. You may state a few of the concepts that are being stressed and how the parent can help at home. You may also leave a short note describing concepts and activities if parents appear ready to participate. If parents are extremely shy, wait for a later visit to talk about educational participation.

■ Help parents understand that their child's success in school is a joint project of the home and school. Encourage their comments and suggestions.

■ Do not overstay. Approximately 30 minutes per visit is best.

■ Do not fill out forms during the visit unless parents are included in the process and told why the information is necessary.

Some parents may make and break appointments repeatedly or will not be home when the teacher arrives. What may at first appear to be disregard for punctuality may be due to parents' self-consciousness about the condition of their home. In other cases, families may be so overwhelmed by problems resulting from poverty, illness, or other situations that they cannot deal with someone coming to their home (Bronfenbrenner 1974). To overcome this problem, some teachers meet parents at a nearby community center or church. An invitation to take the child and the parents to the local ice cream parlor one day after school may also alleviate this situation and will, in addition, serve to satisfy the child that she or he, too, is being visited by the teacher. It may also open communication between parents and teachers so that future visits can take place at home.

Parents can be involved in the child's education at many different levels in varying degrees. A major goal of parent programs should be to involve each individual to an optimal level; for some parents it may be to take on responsibilities at school, while for others only home activities may be possible. The level of home involvement may also vary greatly. Some parents may be able to provide their homes for block or neighborhood meetings while others may only be able to be minimally involved in attending these sessions or having parent-teacher meetings on a one-to-one basis. Still other parents may be only able to work in their own home developing teaching aids to use with their own child. Thus, teachers must be realistic in their expectations.

Teachers and parent program coordinators must also accept the fact that some parents may face too many negative factors in their lives to contribute to a school program in tangible ways. If necessary teachers and parent leaders need to seek ways in which the family may be helped and to recommend agencies or services that are available to them. Communication is even more important in such cases and teachers need to keep in touch with the home about the child's progress through notes and by telephone when available. Even sending home *happy faces* on the child's work is positive communication and lets parents know how the child is doing. Hints on how to help their children at home can also be communicated through notes or newsletters that include instructions on making educational materials or effective ways to interact with young children.

Summary

Effective parent-school programs are based on planning that emphasizes parent involvement to help children toward better achievement in school. Planning a suitable program must include an assessment of needs and resources for a particular school and community.

While sensitivity to parent needs is essential to home-school programs, support for teachers is also vital, for it is ultimately the teachers who are responsible for implementing the major portion of parent involvement programs. The use of community people as liaisons between school and home is recommended as a way to help teachers enhance their interactions with linguistically and culturally different parents. A paid parent coordinator, perhaps a successful teacher in parent-teacher interaction, can direct the program and train teachers to work with parents as well as recruit and orient parents to help them become optimally involved. In a successful program, children will benefit from the combined efforts of school, home, and community.

References

Bauch, J. P.; Vietze, P. M.; and Morris, V. D. "What Makes the Difference in Parental Participation?" *Childhood Education* 50, no. 1 (1973): 47–53.

Berger, E. H. *Parents as Partners in Education: The School and Home Working Together.* St. Louis: Mosby, 1981.

Braun, S. J., and Edwards, E. P. *History and Theory of Early Childhood Education.* Worthington, Ohio: Charles A. Jones, 1972.

Bronfenbrenner, U. *Is Early Intervention Effective?* A Report on Longitudinal Evaluations of Preschool Programs, Vol. 2. Department of Health, Education and Welfare Publication no. (OHD) 76-30025. Washington, D.C.: HEW, 1974.

Croft, D. J. *Parents and Teachers: A Resource Book for Home, School and Community Relations.* Belmont, Calif.: Wadsworth, 1979.

deMause, L., ed. *The History of Childhood.* New York: Harper & Row, 1974.

Escobedo, T. H. "Mexican-American Children and Culture." *Texas Child Care Quarterly* 3, no. 2 (1979): 8–14.

Escobedo, T. H. *Early Childhood Bilingual Education: A Hispanic Perspective.* New York: Teachers College Press, Columbia University, 1983.

Gordon, I. J. *Parent Involvement in Compensatory Education.* Urbana, Ill.: University of Illinois Press, 1970.

Gordon, I. J., and Breivogel, W. F. *Building Effective Home-School Relations.* Boston: Allyn & Bacon, 1976.

Greenwood, G. E.; Breivogel, W. F.; and Bessent, H. "Some Promising Approaches to Parent Involvement." *Theory into Practice* 11 (1972): 183–189.

Laosa, L. "Socialization, Education, and Continuity: The Importance of the Sociocultural Context." *Young Children* 32, no. 5 (July 1977): 21–27.

Lillie, D. L. *Early Childhood Education: An Individualized Approach to Developmental Instruction.* Chicago: Science Research Associates, 1975.

Nedler, S. E., and McAfee, O. D. *Working with Parents: Guidelines for Early Childhood and Elementary Teachers.* Belmont, Calif.: Wadsworth, 1979.

Osborn, D. K. *Early Childhood Education in Historical Perspective.* Athens, Ga.: Education Associates, 1980.

Rodriguez, R. "Levels of Citizen Participation in Selected ESEA Title VII Bilingual Education Advisory Committees." Unpublished doctoral dissertation, University of New Mexico, 1980.

Scriven, G. "Teachers Working with Parents in Schools." *Peabody Journal of Education* 53 (1976): 53–56.

III

Issues in Preparing
Early Childhood
Educators

Olivia N. Saracho
Bernard Spodek

Preparing Teachers for Bilingual/Multicultural Classrooms

The continued healthy development of bilingual/multicultural education is dependent upon the availability of appropriate teaching personnel prepared in high quality colleges and universities. Although in-service programs have always played an important role in preparing bilingual/multicultural teachers, pre-service teacher education programs should become increasingly important.

Teacher education programs are composed of experiences planned to assist prospective teachers in obtaining knowledge and skills essential to teaching. These experiences are based upon research, ethical considerations, and practice. Information is presented here from a variety of sources to identify what we know and consider to be important that can be applied to bilingual/multicultural early childhood teacher education. This component of education cannot be considered separate from education more generally conceived, or from concerns about the development of the children to be taught. Thus, teachers prepared in bilingual/multicultural education must also have the same knowledge, skills, and attitudes expected of all teachers of young children. The six sections that follow parallel six components of a teacher education program identified by Spodek (1969).

Recruitment and selection

Recruiting and selecting prospective teachers are comple-
mentary processes for attracting and evaluating applicants. The
quality and character of early childhood programs are largely
dependent upon the quality and character of the teachers who
staff them. According to Combs (1965), the effective teacher
has:

■ rich, extensive and available perceptions of his/her field
■ precise perceptions of people
■ accurate perceptions of self, leading to adequacy
■ precise perceptions of the purposes and the processes of
learning
■ personal perceptions regarding methods to carry out purposes

Effective teachers should also (Spodek 1969):

■ love and enjoy learning
■ be sensitive to the children's needs and not confuse them
with their own
■ learn which materials are appropriate and should learn to
prepare curriculum
■ possess pleasant and open-ended personalities
■ take pleasure in working with parents

Other important qualities for teachers are warmth, enthusiasm, and a businesslike attitude (Ryans 1960); patience, maturity, energy, encouragement of individual responsibility, and
ingenuity in providing teaching and play materials (Almy
1975); flexibility, warmth, and an ability to enjoy and encourage children (Katz 1969). They should also have the motivation
to teach. Appropriate attitudes for teachers of young children
include an openness to new ideas, some tolerance for ambiguity, an interest in unraveling cause and effect relationships,
and an ability to think and organize data in multidimensional
categories (Almy 1975). Casso and Gonzalez (1974) suggest that
in bilingual/multicultural programs teachers, specifically,
should have additional attributes:

■ the belief that cultural diversity is a worthy goal
■ a respect for the child and the culture he/she brings to
school
■ the conviction that the culture a child brings to school is

worth preserving and enriching
■ an awareness that cultural and linguistic differences are obvious individual differences
■ a commitment to enhance the child's self-image
■ a positive self-concept of the person's ability to contribute to a bilingual/multicultural program
■ a willingness to learn more about bilingual education
■ flexible human relations
■ a capacity to share ideas
■ a confidence in children and their ability to learn

Teachers should have a positive attitude toward all children of any ethnic group, regardless of socioeconomic status, and the belief that all children can learn (Blanco 1975).

There is some disagreement as to whether teachers for bilingual/multicultural programs should be selected from the same ethnic group as the children being taught. Some educators feel that teachers from the same ethnic group provide positive models and encourage students to perform better and may be in a better position to understand and counsel students. Some teachers, however, may be less sensitive and more demanding of children of the same ethnic groups but from a different socioeconomic background, perceiving them as lacking in ability or motivation (Carter 1971).

Bilingual/multicultural programs may deal with a range of languages and cultures. The attitudes, values, and competencies a prospective teacher manifests toward one language and culture may not necessarily transfer to others. Thus, care must be taken to match the teacher to a particular school population. In addition, language and cultural proficiency must become a selection criterion if the program does not train staff in these areas.

The recruitment and selection procedures used for teacher education programs range from open admissions to rigorous selection procedures limiting those who enter the program. Many institutions use academic achievement as measured by high school grades and achievement tests to select students (Lewin and Associates 1977). These criteria, while widely used, may only be remotely related to success in teaching, although certainly basic requirements such as adequate reading ability and verbal communication skills are necessary for teachers.

Turner (1975) advocates motivation as a selection criterion. Those who indicate teaching as their first career choice and

have had prior experiences with young children should be selected. A specific commitment to bilingual/multicultural education might also be required.

Many members of minority groups may not apply to higher
education institutions or even consider the possibility of becoming a teacher. Recruitment methods need to be designed
to attract worthy candidates from many ethnic groups. The
social values and psychological styles of prospective teachers
from varying backgrounds should be given consideration equal
to that of academic achievement. Interpersonal relationships
and healthy self-images are as important as formal academic
skills (Houston and Howsam 1972).

Individuals who are already working with young children,
for example, should be recruited into teacher education programs. Head Start and Follow-Through classes, as well as day
care centers and nursery schools, employ a number of people
from diverse socioeconomic and cultural backgrounds who
may have little formal teacher education but who have demonstrated success in working with young children and their
parents.

General education

Whether in a four-year or a two-year program, general education is basic to all teacher education programs. Teachers
should be well-educated people. Early childhood education is
drawn from various disciplines such as language, social studies,
mathematics, science, aesthetics, and humanities. Simply providing a range of separate subject courses is not an adequate
general education for early childhood teachers. Knowledge
must be integrated and understood to create a broad perspective
and should be made relevant to the general conditions of
human life. The American Association of Colleges for Teacher
Education (1977), in their standards for accreditation of teacher
education programs, suggests that "general education should
include the studies most widely generalizable. General studies
is taught with emphasis upon generalization rather than academic specialization as a primary objective" (p. 4).

General education takes on added importance to teachers of
bilingual/multicultural young children. Teachers need to be
well-grounded in at least two languages and two cultures so

that they can understand the meanings, traditions, and heritage of their future students and thus be better able to guide their learning.

Realms of Meaning (Phenix 1964) can be used to identify the appropriate scope, content, and organization of the general education curriculum related to human nature and knowledge. The first realm, *symbolics*, includes both spoken and written communication. Unique to language is a knowledge of specific sounds, concepts, and grammatical patterns. Language provides a means of understanding and expressing different kinds of experiences and representing the profundity and complexity of the world. Students in bilingual/multicultural early childhood teacher education programs can take language courses related to the target population as well as linguistics.

Through learning a second language, students will also gain insight into a second culture. The traditions, values, customs, symbols, and history of the second culture can be learned through its literature. Literary language allows students to express themselves aesthetically and appreciate the expressions of others.

Knowledge and understanding of *aesthetics*, another realm according to Phenix, provides access to particular perceptions. Each work has its own meaning and speaks for itself. Students can learn to appreciate manufactured and natural objects as well as to express themselves aesthetically through their own work.

Cultural groups vary in their aesthetic values and judgments. Literature, music, dance, and art forms differ from culture to culture. What is considered classic in one culture may be alien to another. Prospective teachers for bilingual/multicultural programs must know the aesthetic elements of the culture about which they are preparing to teach.

Scientific knowledge, Phenix's realm of *empirics*, relates to laws and theories based upon consistent observations which lead to prediction and verification. Science helps in the formulation of valid general descriptions of factual matters by providing information of the world as experienced through measurement. Measurement is used in physical science to develop and test generalizations, laws, and theories.

The social sciences relate to both empirics and the realm of *synnoetics*, and include history, sociology, psychology, and anthropology. History deals with civilization and government and is related to personal and moral knowledge. Events are temporally organized to show the results of decisions which were made during those times studied. Students are encouraged to make predictions and verifications of the historical events by employing different kinds of empirical knowledge as well as personal understanding and ethical insight.

Prospective bilingual/multicultural teachers must know the history of the target cultural groups, their heroes, myths, and contributions to local, national, and world history. Too often minority groups' contributions to the United States have been masked or distorted in social studies textbooks. The social sciences must be presented to students in bilingual/multicultural teacher education in such a way that the general concepts learned can be applied to many cultures and allow for comparisons across cultures. Emphasis, however, should be placed on the cultures in which the teachers will be working and should include not only language, art, history, and music of those cultures, but also social structure and relationships, values, religions, traditions, myths, heroes, and symbols.

Physical education, another area of general education, is composed of intentional activities whose desired effects are communicated through body movement. Health, physical education, and recreation invigorate the human organism and foster neuromuscular skills, good emotional balance and control, and sound judgment. While we often think of the play of young children as universal, different cultures include different play forms and games that teachers should know.

General education can firmly ground the prospective teacher in the culture of the community and the basic structure of the scholarly disciplines. Each community's culture must be known if the teacher is to become a part of it and feel comfortable within it. Each discipline provides a unique point of view, style of thinking, and organization of ideas that contribute to the preparation of teachers.

Professional foundations

Professional foundations are concerned with those aspects of history, philosophy, sociology, economics, psychology, politics, and anthropology that are the basis of education. Linguistics must also be considered a foundation for bilingual/multicultural education. Professional foundations are concerned with a search for knowledge *about* education rather than with professional techniques (Laska 1973; Peters 1977).

In the past, teachers have learned to teach through working with experienced practitioners on the job rather than through the study of educational theory (Peters 1977). Their teaching was based on skilled techniques rather than on knowledge and understanding. Today, theory is presented through foundation courses, which are often eclectic in orientation. These foundation courses should broaden the base of teachers' decisions and actions.

Foundation courses present the world differently from its practical reality (March 1973). Through these courses, prospective teachers are helped to restructure their views of children, school, and subjects; to analyze American educational patterns in relation to democratic ideals; and have a more humanized vision of the education of society (Gillett and Laska 1973). They can help students become more sensitive to how children from different cultural backgrounds have been treated in school, and help students examine and appreciate the aims, ideas, values, influences, and assumptions of a practical education system (Skinner 1968).

Teachers in bilingual/multicultural early childhood education need a broad foundation. They need to become aware of history and traditions of both early childhood education and bilingual/multicultural education. They need to know principles of child growth and development, and of learning theory as well as the cultural, social, and political contexts in which they will be working. They also need to have knowledge of both cultures and both languages as well as of the principles that underlie language and language acquisition—knowledge gained through general education but placed in proper perspective through the foundations.

The foundations of a bilingual/multicultural teacher education program have theoretical and philosophical bases in cultural and linguistic theories and in theories relating to the impact of culture on development. Underlying this should be an understanding and appreciation of the richness of cultural diversity in the United States and the process of cultural diffusion. The potential for both increased culture and value conflict and increased learning opportunities needs to be understood.

The foundations component should lead to a basic understanding of regional, social, and developmental differences in children's language and how culture is reflected in thinking styles, learning styles, and language development. The nature

of bilingualism; the process of becoming bilingual; and the phonological, grammatical, and lexical elements of the two languages involved also need to be imparted. An understanding
of first- and second-language acquisition theory, of the effects
of learning and speaking two languages on the developing child,
and the cultural manifestations related to these language systems will help prospective teachers understand and appreciate
the children they will teach. It will also help the teacher-to-
be better understand and judge various alternative educational
theories and methods.

Instructional knowledge

Instructional knowledge refers to the knowledge that teachers use in classroom practice, planning, and evaluation (Spodek
1969). It involves the selection and sequencing of strategies and
techniques of instruction as well as establishing educational
goals for children.

Teacher roles

An analysis of teachers' roles could provide an alternative
basis for determining the professional knowledge component
of the program. The roles of the teachers include six basic facets.

Decision maker

Teachers plan and implement learning opportunities. They
select from among alternatives and make a range of decisions
about children, materials, activities, and goals. The teacher's
major and most complex role is that of decision maker. One
kind of educational decision includes *policy decisions* related
to the community's values and educational ideologies. These
are decisions about the goals of education, the type of school
supported, and the early childhood curriculum implemented.
A second type includes *institutional decisions* concerned with
the maintenance of the school. These concern classroom organization and the use of physical and human resources. A
third area covers *technical decisions* related to the content and
method of instruction used to accomplish educational goals.
Because children have different learning styles, different teach-

ing methods and content may be necessary in the classroom. The teacher must match methods and materials to children and then evaluate the results of this match (Spodek 1978).

The decision-making role of the teacher of bilingual/multicultural classes is not different from that of other teachers. However, the knowledge that teachers must bring to decision making is much broader because of students and communities with whom they work, the wider range of goals established for bilingual/multicultural programs, and the difficulties in identifying appropriate curriculum models and materials. Curriculum models and materials may have to be adapted to the children's culture. In making decisions, bilingual/multicultural teachers need to be sure that their decisions do not conflict with children's cultures.

Curriculum designer

Teachers need to plan curriculum for young children based upon their capabilities and what is considered important by the community. By considering scope, sequence, and balance the teacher can organize experiences designed to promote learning. Teachers must also consider cultural values, levels of technology, forms of cultural organization, and cultural symbol systems of the school's community so that programs serve social purposes as well as transmit knowledge.

There are four areas of the curriculum particularly important in bilingual/multicultural early childhood education: communication, language expression and acquisition (in both the language the child brings from home and the language of the school), the culture of the home, and the culture of the school. The teacher should create a healthy climate for continued learning in the child's dominant language as well as in a second language. Second-language learning can be related to life in school as well as to life in the community. Since the language children speak will affect their thought patterns and patterns of expression, language instruction in itself is not enough. The curriculum should reflect the cultures of children as well. Children need to be helped to become flexible and adaptable in their thinking and begin to feel comfortable in both cultural worlds.

In formulating educational goals, teachers need to understand the developmental levels of the children with whom they will work as well as their particular educational needs and strengths. They need to be able to work with the local community and with parents to determine expectations for the children's learning. They need to be able to identify and interpret relevant research findings in light of what they know about the children and their community, as well as to put into perspective all influences to determine particular goals.

The curriculum should reflect the similarities and differences between Anglo-American and other cultural and linguistic groups. These should include differences in social structures, in family organizations, in patterns of authority, in language patterns, in knowledge forms, and in art forms. The teacher will also have to be aware of the effects of socioeconomic factors as well as cultural factors on children and on learning. All of this information needs to be processed by the teacher in determining goals.

Broad statements of goals need to be translated into more limited objectives and activities designed to achieve those objectives. Teachers need to be aware of the curriculum models, methods, and materials that are available for bilingual/multicultural early education and judge each one's appropriateness for their particular children. They must know a range of alternative strategies. They need to be aware of the relevant elements of the culture, including language, music, and art that can be included in the curriculum and the resources available in the community to support educational activities related to these elements of culture. Finally, teachers need to know how to organize various resources, both within and outside the classroom, including educational resources, human resources, and cultural resources among others.

Teachers need to be competent in the particular languages and cultures in which they will teach, knowing them well enough to teach in them, as well as to speak and understand intended meanings in the languages. They also need to be versed in techniques of initial- and second-language instruction and be aware of cultural resources and the potential and limitations of these resources. Values assimilated by teachers can directly affect the types of materials they use with young children and the kinds of behavior they reward or restrict.

Especially in bilingual/multicultural early childhood classes, the teacher's activities need to extend beyond the classroom. Working with parents is an important part of the curriculum. The teacher needs to help parents with their resources for children, while involving them in basic decisions about the children's program.

Organizer of instruction

Teachers can use long-range and short-range planning to put these resources to their best use. Teachers need to consider children's interests, capacities, limitations, and aspirations to successfully arrange activity schedules, organize children into workable groups, and arrange classroom materials and equipment to make the best use of space. Teachers should help children use learning resources both inside and outside the school.

Advance planning helps teachers anticipate what materials and resources will be necessary for instruction. Specific goals for each child can be identified in advance, and a variety of activities presented to help children meet their needs within the program. Adequate planning can ensure the availability of legitimate learning alternatives. The careful selection and integration of materials and resources which are relevant from both a language and cultural point of view should assume a high priority.

The materials that teachers need for a bilingual/multicultural class may not always be available through traditional sources. Teachers will have to learn about alternative sources, and how to adapt materials designed for more mature audiences, as well as be able to create their own original material when appropriate.

Too often teachers in bilingual/multicultural programs feel that, while other parts of the program can be presented indirectly through activities, language instruction should be sequenced formally and presented directly (Saville and Troike 1975). However, indirect instruction through activities can also be used for teaching language. Children can be allowed to move freely from one activity to another, and this freedom of movement could characterize language activities. Conceptually enriching activities that allow children to assimilate expressive and receptive language skills in a naturalistic fashion can be provided (John 1970).

There is a wide range of first- and second-language instructional strategies available that teachers must learn. They need to be able to individualize their program using inquiry/discovery techniques and independent activities as well as direct instruction. Learning to use audio-visual devices and organizing the classroom into learning centers can help teachers use these techniques.

Teachers need to be able to teach in both languages in all

areas of the curriculum using the local dialect and incorporating specific linguistic and cultural elements of the community into the instructional program. This will help the children to maintain their cultural identification and pride in their background and heritage.

Many adults are involved in the education of young children including principals, center directors, head teachers, teacher-directors, classroom teachers, teacher aides, teachers' assistants, and volunteers. All must be made aware of the school's philosophy and have their specific roles, responsibilities, and expectations explained.

Parents are particularly important to the program. Teachers may have to provide instruction to parents so that school learnings can be extended into the home. They may also have to learn how to learn from parents, who know a great deal about the language and culture of a specific community.

Diagnostician

Teachers must assess the capabilities and limitations of the children and select teaching techniques based upon what the children can and need to achieve. A range of child study techniques are used by teachers to better understand the child, including observation, informal and formal tests, anecdotal records, and collections of samples of children's work. Observation includes recording direct observations of the flow of behavior as well as the use of structured scales and checklists. A number of standardized tests which have been demonstrated to be somewhat reliable and valid are available for use with young children. These tests provide only a limited amount of information that teachers need to know. Many standardized tests are not appropriate for children of all language and cultural backgrounds. Informal testing, which could consist of asking children to respond to a set of predetermined questions orally or to demonstrate a specific behavior, can be helpful in providing the information a teacher specifically desires (Goodwin and Driscoll 1980).

Teachers of bilingual/multicultural young children need to know about tests and other assessment devices and should be aware of the cultural and linguistic biases that exist in many of them. They need to match their assessment to their students and to program goals. They must know the appropriate tests and informal assessment tools that exist, as well as how to use them, for identifying both the children's levels of educational achievement and language competence both in their dominant language and in their second language.

As diagnosticians, teachers should be as much concerned with acceptance as with assessment. The fact that the bilingual child's home language is different from the language of the school might lead the teacher to overlook important strengths that could be used to further learning. Each child, however, comes to class with a range of previously acquired concepts, skills, and understandings. Each child comes with competence in some language, complete with a sound system, grammar, and vocabulary (Saville and Troike 1975). The early childhood teacher should be able to diagnose the language competency of each child as well as be able to relate what the child has previously learned to what is expected in school (Casso and Gonzalez 1974).

Whatever diagnostic techniques are used, teachers need to be careful that the information collected provides a representative picture of the child, even though it is only a limited sample of behavior.

Manager of learning

Placing a group of 15, 20, or more children in a single classroom for many hours each day can cause problems if proper management is neglected. Children learn at different rates and vary in their competencies. Children have different cognitive styles, interests, and needs. Ignoring individual differences and teaching only to the average, expecting the other children to adjust to this situation, creates educational disadvantages and castigates children for being different. Providing children with a wide variety of learning alternatives is one way of coping with this individual and group conflict. Using prescribed activities may increase the conflict between individual and group needs.

The teacher's management role includes creating an attractive educational environment in the classroom and planning and implementing educational and cultural activities. Teachers should establish work routines, present subject matter, and provide educational tools and classroom displays which are appropriate to the children's age level, interests, and culture (Eddy 1969).

Management problems can arise during transition times, when students return from recess or when they move from one activity to another. Children complete their work at different rates and a few cannot always be expected to wait for the rest of the class. Difficulties may also be caused by boredom, an insistence on conformity, a failure to orient some children, unclearly defined tasks, and a possible fear of failure. Requiring children to clean up, line up, move from one area to another, or wait can cause problems. Teachers have to cope with these situations, becoming aware of which children have problems and providing special support for them during transition. Anticipating transition problems and preparing for them can prevent unmanageable situations (Spodek 1978). During and after transition periods, several techniques must be implemented to reestablish a manageable condition in which children can proceed with their educational work. These methods facilitate teaching performance (Eddy 1969).

Counselor/adviser

Teachers have a responsibility to assist each child in acquiring desirable behaviors, learning to deal with others, and coping with feelings. Effective teachers must be involved both personally and professionally in the educational process. Teachers can instruct, coach, and model to achieve these ends, constantly interacting with children during the day, providing caretaking, emotional support, and guidance as well as instruction. The classroom atmosphere should be designed to create a sense of trust and security. Children's strengths and weaknesses must be accepted and their sociocultural backgrounds respected.

Success in learning is dependent upon motivation to learn. Motivation grows from becoming aware of the importance and relevance of what is being learned as well as from developing self-confidence. With a positive self-image and a sense of affectance, children become more willing to accept challenges, take risks in learning new things, and test themselves in new situations.

Teachers must help motivate children. They must also be particularly sensitive to the culture and language that pupils bring to school. Language and culture are very much a part of each individual's self. How one values language and culture reflects how one values individuals. Teachers need to support the children's own life pursuits, nurturing their feeling of self-worth. Academic competence should never be achieved at the expense of a child's personal feeling of self-worth.

Providing support for the child as a person requires that teachers extend themselves by making contact with parents and community members, providing support in the home and community for the school's programs as well as providing support within the school for the activities of the home and community. In this way teachers can support the child's development to become an integrated person based on the experiences gained in two cultural contexts.

Teachers need to reinforce what has been taught in the home. For example, the Mexican-American family makes very young children, especially the youngest one in the family, feel they are the most important person in the world. This enhances their self-concept and builds their trust in adults. The teacher needs to make these children feel important but at the same time teach them to make realistic judgments about their worth. In the Mexican-American culture, the child is taught to have a deep consideration for others and to provide a great deal of warmth. A child who finds a teacher cold and distant may encounter culture shock.

Practice

According to Dearden (1968), there are three kinds of learned concepts:

1. perceptual concepts about physical objects and properties
2. practical concepts about how people use the objects in their culture
3. theoretical concepts which are the intellectual concepts transmitted in the process of knowledge and understanding

Prospective teachers learn practical concepts as they attempt to apply theory in a practice situation with help and guidance from cooperating teachers and college supervisors (Tibble 1971).

The use of field experiences to integrate previous learning with emerging experiences transforms theoretical instruction into reality (Borrowman 1965). The practice component should use intellectual methods to understand the nature of good practice as well as provide opportunities to improve practice. An overemphasis on field experiences to the exclusion of other program components may move teacher education toward a nonintellectual apprenticeship program. If only the practical is emphasized, basic theories and a merging of ideas with practice may be overlooked or undervalued (Gillett 1973).

The practice component of the teacher education program includes field experiences such as workshops, observations, simulations, practica, and student teaching. Workshops allow students to present and practice teaching techniques with different types of materials and to study effects of these techniques on children. A workshop may consist of constructing children's equipment, presenting a movement and dance session, painting or sculpting, experimenting with science materials, designing and using puppets, or exploring new materials (Almy 1975).

Classroom observation allows the students to see teachers in action and relate observations of practice to theory. Sensitive observing allows a student or teacher to recognize the significant clues that lead to an understanding of the event and allows inferences to be made and responses planned based on something more than intuition.

In simulation, students play a hypothetical role in a simple and controlled situation. In microteaching, a form of simulation, the prospective teacher presents a short activity to a small group of children which is later viewed, analyzed, and evaluated. The interest or boredom of the children in an activity can be observed, for example, to provide an index of its effectiveness (Almy 1975).

Early experiences can be integrated with foundations courses through activities such as visits to school board meetings, conferences with officials or teacher's unions, and meetings with parents and members of child advocacy groups. Early experiences with children can also allow student teachers to develop greater responsibility and self-confidence (Borrowman 1965).

Field experiences can improve prospective teachers' performances as they learn about the importance of teacher-pupil relationships and observe children in a variety of circumstances (Borrowman 1965). Field experiences, unfortunately, may also negatively affect attitudes and behaviors of prospective teachers who may become more authoritarian, rigid, controlling, restrictive, impersonal, and custodial; and less pupil centered, accepting, and humanistic if this is what they experience in the field (Peck and Tucker 1973; Katz 1974). Thus, it is essential that prospective teachers be exposed to high-quality field placements.

Student teaching is a culminating experience, and should be as nearly like teaching as possible. While student teaching, students should attend regular seminars which allow them to share their experiences and work out their problems in a group. These seminars should be conducted to promote intellectual growth and professional socialization. The supervisor can also have individual conferences with the students and cooperating teacher to provide additional opportunities beyond the seminar.

Field experiences play a special role in relation to bilingual/multicultural early childhood education. College classes can present only a limited picture of reality. Field placements can help students develop insights into the language and culture of the children they will be teaching. The practice component of a bilingual/multicultural teacher education program should include experiences beyond the school, in homes and communities of the target culture. It also should provide students with direct contact with bilingual/multicultural programs of high quality in schools.

Bilingual/multicultural education is in a relatively early stage of development in the United States. Students need to have direct contact with a variety of approaches to teaching, materials, and program models. By working with bilingual/multicultural children in a class with a teacher, being given increasing amounts of responsibility, and being given continuous feedback on performance, future teachers will learn about educational practices and will become proficient in them. They will be better able to understand the meaning of college coursework as it is reflected and integrated in practice.

Program modification

Program modification is an essential component for any teacher education program because it provides for program improvement through evaluation. Stake (1971) identifies the three goals of educational evaluation:

■ to foster an understanding of the current status of the educational system
■ to provide data for the correction of shortcomings
■ to move the never-ending evolution of the curriculum toward a better balance among the rational, the intuitive, and the humane

There are different ways to evaluate teacher education programs:

■ Programs of education and teacher education are based upon specific ideals and values, whether or not these ideals and values are made explicit. These determine the judgment of what treatments are considered worthy and what outcomes are considered worthy for each program.

■ Program treatments can be portrayed to determine whether treatment elements are consistent with values and expected outcomes.

■ Program outcomes can be assessed in terms of their consistency with program ideals and values as well as with the context in which the teacher is operating. Indicators of outcomes may vary for different types of programs.

■ Programs of teacher education can be compared on common dimensions (Spodek 1975).

Program evaluation requires information on its worth, practicality, and effectiveness. The worth of a program relates to both the underlying values of the program and the evaluator's values. The program's practical aspects can be assessed by observing the degree to which activities are generated that are consistent with the program's intentions. The program's effectiveness is supported with evidence about outcomes.

There are different ways to evaluate programs. Most programs use preordinate evaluations, which depend on prespecification of goals, tests of student performance, and a research-type report. Responsive evaluation can be used in place of preordinate evaluation.

Responsive evaluation focuses on program experiences rather than program intents. It assesses what people do naturally. Observations and reactions are the major means of collecting data. The evaluator observes the perceptions and values of individuals, examines records, and presents a report formally or informally, orally or in writing, and in different forms such as brief narratives, portrayals, product displays, or graphs, depending upon the needs of the audience. The evaluator's major responsibility is to provide sufficient information through various means about the program in order that others have a basis for making decisions. It is not the role of the evaluator to make a judgment about changing a program. The evaluator has insufficient knowledge as to the program's functioning or the consequences of the judgment. In addition, if the evaluator assumes the role of judge, the availability of data might decrease (Stake 1974; 1976).

Teacher education programs should include both internal and external evaluation. The internal evaluation can be conducted by the staff and could consist of group sessions, conferences, observations, and a monitoring of program elements. Information about what is actually happening in the program could be thus collected. The purpose of this evaluation would be to broaden the staff's perception of the program and to clarify the staff's perception of the program and the staff's concerns regarding issues and values.

Staff members are often too involved in a program to be objective (Scriven 1973). An external evaluator, a person with broader perspective who can be trusted by students and staff, could be used to provide this objectivity. The external evaluation could be extensive, with the evaluator making regular visits to the program to collect data for a good part of the academic year. Program documents such as students' personal files, samples of students' work, inventories, the curriculum guides, syllabus, and staff meeting reports could be examined. Group sessions, student conferences, classes, practicum sites, and staff meetings could be observed. Student files could be reviewed to provide evidence to be verified by procedures such as observation.

Evaluation could also make use of participants' perceptions of the program. This is one measure of program effectiveness that can be assessed directly or indirectly. Interviews or questionnaires could be used to collect data, but should not be trusted blindly (Cronbach 1972).

The evaluation of a bilingual/multicultural teacher education program requires teacher educators to judge the integration of content related to bilingualism and multiculturalism within all aspects of the program as well as judging the outcomes of the program: the preparation of teachers competent to work in those bilingual/multicultural classes for which the program is designed. It is helpful to include members of the target community in the evaluation team in gathering information and making judgments. They can bring sensitivity and competence to the evaluation that will enlarge the perspective of the teacher education community.

Teachers can have a long-lasting influence on the young children in their classes. Teacher competence must be rooted in an understanding of children and culture and in a set of values that determines the kinds of influences we want to have on children. Thus, all aspects of a teacher education program must be considered in designing a program to prepare teachers of bilingual/multicultural young children.

References

Almy, M. *The Early Childhood Educator at Work.* New York: McGraw-Hill, 1975.

American Association of Colleges for Teacher Education. *Standards and Evaluative Criteria for the Accreditation of Teacher Education: A Draft of the Proposed New Standards with Study Guide.* Washington, D.C.: AACTE, 1977.

Blanco, G. M. "La Preparacion de Profesores Bilingues." In *Proceedings of the First Inter-American Conference on Bilingual Education,* ed. R. C. Troike and N. Modiano. Reston, Va.: Center for Applied Linguistics, 1975.

Borrowman, M. L. *Teacher Education in America.* New York: Teachers College Press, 1965.

Carter, T. P. "Mexican-Americans in School: A History of Educational Neglect." In *Teaching Multicultural Populations: Five Heritages,* ed. J. C. Stone and D. P. DeNevi. New York: Van Nostrand, 1971.

Casso, H., and Gonzalez, D. "Bilingual Bicultural Education: A Challenge to the Open Classroom Unit." In *A Manual Prepared for the Teacher Training Institute.* Westport, Conn.: Mediax Associates, 1974.

Combs, A. W. *The Professional Preparation of Teachers.* Boston: Allyn & Bacon, 1965.

Cronbach, L. J. "Course Improvement Through Evaluation." In *Readings in Curriculum Evaluation,* ed. P. A. Taylor and D. M. Cowley. Dubuque, Iowa: Brown, 1972.

Dearden, R. F. *The Philosophy of Primary Education.* London: Routledge & Kegan Paul, 1968.

Eddy, E. M. *Becoming a Teacher.* New York: Teachers College Press, 1969.

Gillett, M. "Introduction to New Directions." In *Foundation Studies in Education: Justifications and New Directions,* ed. J. A. Laska and M. Gillett. Metuchen, N. J.: The Scarecrow Press, 1973.

Gillett, M., and Laska, J. A., eds. *Foundation Studies in Education: Justifications and New Directions.* Metuchen, N.J.: The Scarecrow Press, 1973.

Goodwin, W. A., and Driscoll, L. A. *Handbook for Measurement and Evaluation in Early Childhood Education.* San Francisco: Jossey-Bass, 1980.

Houston, W. R., and Howsam, R. B. *Competency-Based Teacher Education: Progress, Problems, and Prospects.* Chicago: Science Research Associates, 1972.

John, V. P. "Cognitive Development in the Bilingual Child." In *Bilingualism and Language Contact*, ed. J. E. Alatis. Washington, D.C.: Georgetown University Press, 1970.

Katz, L. G. "Issues and Problems in Education." In *Teacher Education: of the Teacher, by the Teacher, for the Child*, ed. B. Spodek. Washington, D.C.: National Association for the Education of Young Children, 1974.

Katz, L. G. *Teaching in Preschools: Roles and Goals*. Urbana, Ill.: ERIC Clearinghouse on Early Childhood Education, 1969.

Laska, J. A. "Introduction to Perspectives on Foundation Studies." In *Foundation Studies in Education: Justifications and New Directions*, ed. J. A. Laska and M. Gillett. Metuchen, N.J.: The Scarecrow Press, 1973.

Lewin and Associates. *The State of Teacher Education, 1977*. Washington, D.C.: U.S. Department of Health, Education and Welfare, n.d.

March, L. "Generic and Specific Contributions of Sociology to Teacher Education." In *Foundation Studies in Education: Justifications and New Directions*, ed. J. A. Laska and M. Gillett. Metuchen, N.J.: The Scarecrow Press, 1973.

Peck, R. F., and Tucker, J. A. "Research on Teacher Education." In *Second Handbook of Research on Teaching*, ed. R.M.W. Travers. Chicago: Rand McNally, 1973.

Peters, R. S. *Education and the Education of Teachers*. Boston: Routledge & Kegan Paul, 1977.

Phenix, P. H. *Realms of Meaning*. New York: McGraw-Hill, 1964.

Ryans, D. G. *Characteristics of Teachers*. Washington, D.C.: American Council on Education, 1960.

Saville, M. R., and Troike, R. C. *A Handbook of Bilingual Education*. Washington, D.C.: Teachers of English to Speakers of Other Languages, 1975.

Scriven, M. "Goal-Free Evaluation." In *School Evaluation: The Politics and Process*, ed. E. T. House. Berkeley, Calif.: McCutchan, 1973.

Skinner, A. F. "Teacher-Training and the Foundational Studies." *Teacher Education* 19, no. 1 (1968): 26–38.

Spodek, B. "Early Childhood Education and Teacher Education: A Search for Consistency." *Young Children* 30, no. 3 (March 1975): 168–173.

Spodek, B. "Constructing a Model for a Teacher Education Program in Early Childhood Education." *Contemporary Education* 40 (1969): 145–149.

Spodek, B. *Teaching in the Early Years*. 2nd. ed. Englewood Cliffs, N.J.: Prentice-Hall, 1978.

Stake, R. E. *The Evaluation of College Teaching: A Position Paper*. Urbana, Ill.: University of Illinois, 1971.

Stake, R. E. *SAFARI Project: Safari, Innovation, Evaluation, Re-*

search and the Problem of Control: Some Interim Papers. Norwich, England: Center for Applied Research in Education, University of East Anglia, 1974.

Stake, R. E. *Evaluating Educational Programmes: The Need and the Response.* Paris: Organisation for Economic Cooperation and Development, 1976.

Tibble, J. W. "The Organization and Supervision of School Practice." In *The Future of Teacher Education,* ed. J. W. Tibble. London: Routledge & Kegan Paul, 1971.

Turner, R. L. "An Overview of Research in Teacher Education." In *Teacher Education, 74th Yearbook of the National Society for the Study of Education,* ed. K. Ryan, Chicago: The University of Chicago Press, 1975.

Dean C. Corrigan

10
Education and Human Services Delivery

S ociety faces one of its most pressing problems today in building a better nation—improving the quality and opportunity of education for students with special needs. As Cremin of Columbia Teachers College stated at a 1976 Congressional hearing, "Any system of universal education is ultimately tested at its margin, what is or is not done for the education of those most in need, those who have hitherto stood on the periphery of our concerns, will determine the effectiveness of the entire system." Schools or early childhood centers and the educators who staff them are the primary instrument in effecting social change. While a growing number of educational programs are persisting in efforts to develop humane, individualized, and socially responsive climates, the majority have not made changes in purpose, substance, or form. Teachers need support from parents, child advocates, and legislators, as well as an environment that enhances professional practice, to perform their complex social and educational functions.

Schools, teachers, and teaching

Many schools in both high- and low-socioeconomic status (SES) areas are structured to produce *winners* and *losers*. Students' performances are judged against a preconceived standard or against the average of their class rather than viewed as achievement in relation to abilities. None of us as adults would continue to play a game we had no chance of winning, yet we expect students to do this everyday in school.

Too many schools and centers for young children are run like custodial institutions. Because they usually have overwhelming numbers of students and limited resources for individual attention, custodial institutions organize and control life by rigid regulation and routines to defend themselves. Custodial institutions maintain close surveillance at all times to minimize incidents and to ensure compliance. Even the physical environment is structured for control, for example, classrooms and isolation in time-out places. Because custodial institutions tend to assume that everyone in them needs to be controlled, there is little time left for those who have learned to make choices and be responsible for them, or for creating conditions that help all involved to learn to make choices—and deal with the consequences. This kind of dehumanizing environment appears in educational institutions, destroying motivation for children and leaving them with no sense of respect for teachers or sense of responsibility for the success of themselves or their classmates.

America's schools have been caught in the dilemma of their posture toward reform and preservation. The local and governmental charges of the past have caused schools to be conservative and preservative. And, up to now, the organized teaching profession also has been past-oriented, partly because of its own disposition and partly because it had to be if it was to have public support and acceptance. The teaching profession has rarely chosen to challenge parents in favor of a more suitable school situation for their children.

As a result, schools have remained a place for safe ideas. Adopted curriculum backed by publicly screened textbooks and materials have kept bounds on social thought. Within the schoolhouse doors, controversial issues are deliberately avoided. Even though children are confronted everyday in the media and in their personal lives with the problems of discrimination, drugs, sex, poverty, war, pollution, energy, injustice, and corruption, schools do not deal with these persistent life situations in ways that help children to make intelligent decisions.

In this context, it is no wonder that the public image of the teacher does not match the importance of the role. Lortie (1975) suggests that

> teaching seems to have more than its share of status anomalies. It is honored and disdained, praised as "dedicated service" and lampooned as "easy work." It is permeated with the rhetoric of

professionalism, yet features incomes below those earned by workers with considerably less education . . . . Teaching from its inception in America has occupied a special but shadowed social standing . . . real regard shown for those who taught has never matched professed regard. (p. 2)

It is unfortunate that many teachers and teacher educators accept low public assessments of the teaching profession's worth. Too many teachers view themselves as clerks and technicians, rather than professionals:

The tragedy is that most people do not recognize the life and death nature of teaching . . . . Every moment in the lives of teachers and pupils brings critical decisions of motivation, reinforcement, reward, ego enhancement, and goal direction. Proper professional decisions enhance learning and life; improper decisions send the learner towards incremental death in openness to experience and in ability to learn and contribute. Doctors and lawyers probably have neither more nor less to do with life, death and freedom than do teachers. To deny the child the skills and qualities of the fully professional teacher exacerbates the assaults on freedom which much of mass education renders inevitable, and leaves to chance the kinds of interventions by teachers that open minds and enhance self-images. Therefore, the teaching profession must continue its negotiations with society in behalf of more perfect education for its children. Teaching is definitely a matter of life and death. It should be entrusted only to the most thoroughly prepared professionals. (Howsam et al. 1976, pp. 26–28)

Improving teacher education

The creation of new kinds of schools depends on the development of new programs of teacher education to prepare new professionals capable of implementing these reforms. Comprehensive change must take place in colleges as well as schools. Here are some aspects of teacher education which must be redesigned.

Life space

If teacher educators are to provide the essential knowledge and skill to pre-service students, then they will need the life space to do so. *Life space* refers to the resources often in short supply in many teacher education programs such as time, facilities, personnel, instructional and research materials, and access to quality instruction in academic units.

Across the country, today's teachers are certified and placed in service with only a minimum of professional preparation. What is needed is a protracted program of professional education similar to those in other professions. The program should extend the training period from four to five years. It should also add, as a critical part of teacher preparation, a sixth year internship.

Licensing should be awarded only after this period of demonstrated competence (internship) under the supervision of a mentor and/or local review board of professional peers. In New York and Ohio, state commissions have already submitted proposals for five-year programs. Also, many other state units of the American Association of Colleges for Teacher Education are studying five- and six-year patterns of preparation.

Knowledge base

Once the life space is provided, teacher education can identify and teach the valid knowledge base needed by teachers to ensure competence prior to professional teaching. Teaching is an applied *science*. The difference between an educated person and a professional teacher is *pedagogy*—the science of teaching. Teacher education is a process which transforms educated individuals from lay citizens to professional educators; the role performance of teachers is importantly altered during the preparation process.

The complexities of teaching require rigorous pre-service preparation. Teachers need to be well-educated in liberal or general studies, since *all* teachers are teachers of general education. Teachers also require intensive preparation in the conceptual frameworks and underlying principles on which they will base professional decisions. A broad repertoire of teaching behaviors and skills, incorporating both theoretical and experiential components, must be learned.

To assist pre-service students in relating generic skills and theoretical components to specific community and school needs, preparation programs should provide options for every student to study in depth at least one local, regional, or national subculture.

Prospective teachers must have a solid background in the basic disciplines of education, including psychology, sociology, anthropology, and philosophy. However, changes must be made in these areas too such as emphasis on theory as applied to practice.

Meeting the needs of education students

The uniqueness of individuals and their learning needs should determine goals for teacher educators. From this learner-centered base, students may then set their own personal and professional goals and organize specific approaches to these goals with advice from other teachers in preparation and teacher-educators. This approach contrasts sharply with the approach that starts with someone else's long list of teacher competencies. The program should be competency-based but the competencies should emerge from activity with the learner in the school and community where the relevance of the performance goals become personally legitimized by the prospective teacher.

Knowledge as means

Memorizing detailed information and didactic material is of little use to teachers. Knowledge about the educative process, the nature of children and youth, subject matter, the educational setting including school and society, the nature of teaching, and instructional materials and media cannot be taught meaningfully when isolated from the complex problems to which they are to be applied. All dimensions of teacher education—liberal arts, specialization in a discipline or broad fields, professional studies, and personal study of the self can be integrated if they are offered throughout the lifetime career of teachers while they are both studying and practicing new ways that education can improve the human condition.

We need to ask whether the knowledge we are offering to prospective teachers is appropriate to the community they are entering, and whether the community is a humane community. If it is not, then they should have the skills, understandings, and desire to change things. The goal of *social* self-actualization—developing people who can learn and work together—must be coupled with the goal of fostering *self*-actualization. Social growth toward a healthy community and self-development are equally important. Prospective teachers will have to be educated to be toughminded and capable of dealing with the politics of school and community change and with the unexpected.

A look into the future indicates that teachers and other educational personnel will perform a broad range of human services operating from community-school centers: they may be street workers; they may teach in settings which involve children and parents; they will relate to social services personnel in corrections, mental health, and rehabilitation agencies; they will be part of a team whose goal is to create healthy human communities. Indeed, the range of personnel educated by the reformed programs will probably be as broad as the needs of the communities served.

The goal we must set for colleges of education is to develop skills in how to *use* knowledge. Knowledge for its own sake was once thought to be, and still is in some places, the mark of a true intellectual. Basic science was defined as that which would not yet be applied; it almost came to mean science whose consequences one does not need to be concerned about. The belief in knowledge for its own sake has diverted increasing amounts of student and faculty time away from solving present problems, and creating a better future.

A new strategy for reform

The strategy for improving schools through teacher education in the past was to prepare new teachers with the most recent knowledge in their field, and new techniques for individualizing instruction, and send them out to improve the schools. This strategy has failed—new teachers and their ideas have been swallowed up by the system. The teachers now in the schools who are 40 to 45 years old have 20 to 25 years of teaching left. Unless we reeducate them with the new teachers, schools will not improve significantly. In a world whose most constant characteristic is change, teachers more than other professionals must keep up to date on knowledge in their field as well as ways to improve teaching and learning. The major educational challenge facing this country in the next five years is to reeducate one and one-half million experienced teachers and it cannot be done between 8:00 and 8:30 in the morning or between 4:00 and 5:00 in the afternoon.

We must develop a new approach to teacher education. We

need a strategy which brings together pre-service and in-service teachers in the same training program in a team relationship. The program should have as its primary goal the improvement of all aspects of educating children. Training can be developed as part of a joint search for better ways to improve educational care. From this cooperative school-college commitment, the training program will receive its relevance and its vitality.

There is a great deal of talk about collaboration today. Those of us who are teacher educators should be clear at the outset about what collaboration will mean if we move in the afore-mentioned directions. If school districts are going to assist in financing the reeducation of teachers, the program must be designed in such a way that it helps teachers solve instructional problems they face. This implies that much more training will take place on-site with as many teachers as possible enrolled from the same school. In this approach, new ideas can be tested in the environment from which the problems and the attending teacher education curriculum emerged. If, after a period of time, the training program does not improve the learning environment, it can be changed or replaced with another program. Colleges of education will become relevant and useful, or cease to exist. Furthermore, we must go beyond the schools in meeting the educational needs of our citizens.

If our colleges are to become powerful instruments for social progress, we will need a new design for programs to prepare human services professionals. Instead of a *schooling system*, we need a *human service delivery system*. Our colleges, working together, must become the training and research arm of that delivery system. Resources, both financial and personal, must be directed toward strategies that link schools and social agencies with colleges. Shuffling courses about is not the answer. A new philosophy in form and substance is needed with an organizational structure that links us to our professional constituencies. Central to this design is a new partnership among agencies operating at different phases of the human service delivery system. We can no longer live in splendid isolation. We need to recognize the fact that pre-service, continuing, or in-service education; schools and social agencies; and universities and colleges are each an interacting component of *one* human service delivery system.

The new design for human service delivery should emerge from the basic premise that the most significant interaction that takes place in any kind of helping relationship is a teaching-learning component. One of the most exciting things that is happening to some colleges of education is that they are becoming colleges of education and *social services*. They are moving toward an organizational approach that conceives of everyone who comes into the college as a human service educator. The human service educator notion becomes the umbrella under which all subject areas and programs are integrated. Are there real differences in the competencies and skills that you need to do counseling in a corrections center, or school, or senior citizens center, or hospital? If our goal is to improve learning environments in homes as well as in community action centers, museums, schools, industry, or senior citizens homes, then we need a conceptual base and an educational design that provides the opportunity to work through and influence the whole of society.

The human service educator concept is enhanced further by the emergence of a learning society in which no one ever completes an education. A formal educational structure must be available to all citizens of all ages in a society such as ours where jobs become obsolete and facts meaningless and where change and the insecurities of a changing society are promised as a way of life. The learning force has exceeded the work force. Professional colleges must now talk about *staffing the learning society* not just staffing schools.

The education profession can take the initiative in moving the concept of human service educator forward by developing collaborative programs across the human service professions. Only when educators see society, not just the classroom, as a learning place, in which teaching is a vital function will our profession reach maturity.

Conclusion

There has been a great deal of talk and emotion about advocacy and political action. This dialogue is long overdue within the profession. However, it will be counterproductive unless it is followed with action. We have raised the expectations of the needy too many times and have produced dashed hopes too often.

In a political action network, we must include other professionals who work with children. Child advocates must start working together as *one profession* for our clients to convince the public to spend less for defense and more for children—our greatest resource.

The greatest challenge facing educators in the days ahead is to convince public officials in local, state, and federal agencies that a nation that evades the responsibility of providing resources to educate its citizens does nothing for itself in the long run. Unless we convince the public, *and the profession*, that the education of other peoples' children is as important as the education of their own, the concept of access to equal opportunity for all will not become a reality.

If the teaching profession is to be visionary, it must also be responsible. We are responsible for the environment we leave for those who live after us. We can destroy it and them or, as is shown by the recent increase in depression among children, we can destroy their hope and happiness.

The most severe shortcoming of our educational and social services programs is that we have concentrated on means rather than ends. Too often, we maintain the illusion of neutrality. Those who hope that education can be completely objective are confused. A value-free education cannot exist. Educators must choose to be conscious and positive about values. We must ask, "How can we best use our time to serve the public interest?" We are not faced with an insoluble problem. Nor, however, are we dealing with a problem that minor tinkering will correct:

> What the teaching profession needs is a totally new set of concepts regarding the nature of the emerging human services society, its educational demands, the kinds of delivery systems necessary to provide public access to continuing educational opportunity, and the types of professional personnel and training required to reform public education. (Howsam et al. 1976, p. 138)

The new teaching profession must create the future.

References

Lortie, D. *Schoolteacher: A Sociological Study.* Chicago: The University of Chicago Press, 1975.

Howsam, R.; Corrigan, D.; Denemark, G.; and Nash, R. *Educating a Profession.* Bicentennial Commission Report on Education for the Profession of Teaching. Washington, D.C.: American Association of Colleges for Teacher Education, 1976.

List of contributors

Bradford Chambers
Editor, *Interracial Books for
Children Bulletin*
Council on Interracial Books
for Children
1841 Broadway
New York, NY 10023

Dean C. Corrigan
Dean
College of Education
Texas A & M University
College Station, TX 77843

Theresa Herrera Escobedo
Director
Project for Minorities and
Women in Research
Department of Curriculum
and Instruction
University of Texas
Austin, TX 78712

Rosario C. Gingras
Center for Applied Linguistics
3520 Prospect St., N.W.
Washington, DC 20007

Janice Hale
Associate Professor
Department of Early
Childhood/Elementary
Education
Jackson State University
Jackson, MS 39209

Frances Martinez Hancock
Director
Champaign County Child
Development Center
1203 W. Green St.
Urbana, IL 61801

Margie K. Kitano
Associate Professor
Department of Educational
Specialties
New Mexico State University
La Cruces, NM 88003

Jeanne B. Morris
Associate Professor
Illinois State University
Department of Curriculum
and Instruction
Normal, IL 61761

Olivia N. Saracho
Associate Professor
Department of Early
Childhood/Elementary
Education
University of Maryland
College Park, MD 20742

Bernard Spodek
Professor
Early Childhood Education
University of Illinois
1310 S. 6th St.
Champaign, IL 61820

Terry Tafoya
Northwest Institute for Native
Education
5715 N. E. 65th St.
Seattle, WA 98115

Information about
NAEYC

NAEYC is . . .

. . . a membership supported organization of people committed to fostering the growth and development of children from birth through age eight. Membership is open to all who share a desire to serve and act on behalf of the needs and rights of young children.

NAEYC provides . . .

. . . educational services and resources to adults who work with and for children, including

- *Young Children, the* Journal for early childhood educators
- **Books, posters,** and **brochures** to expand your knowledge and commitment to young children, with topics including infants, curriculum, research, discipline, teacher education, and parent involvement
- An **Annual Conference** that brings people from all over the country to share their expertise and advocate on behalf of children and families
- **Week of the Young Child** celebrations sponsored by NAEYC Affiliate Groups across the country to call public attention to the needs and rights of children and families
- **Insurance plans** for individuals and programs
- **Public policy information** for informed advocacy efforts at all levels of government

For free information about membership, publications, or other NAEYC services . . .

. . . call NAEYC toll free at 800-424-2460 or 202-232-8777 or write to NAEYC, 1834 Connecticut Ave., N.W., Washington, DC 20009.